The POWER Series

Desert Storm
SEA WAR

Arnold Meisner

Motorbooks International
Publishers & Wholesalers

First published in 1991 by Motorbooks International
Publishers & Wholesalers, PO Box 2, 729 Prospect
Avenue, Osceola, WI 54020 USA

The information in this book is true and complete to
the best of our knowledge. All recommendations are
made without any guarantee on the part of the
author or Publisher, who also disclaim any liability
incurred in connection with the use of this data or
specific details

We recognize that some words, model names and
designations, for example, mentioned herein are the
property of the trademark holder. We use them for
identification purposes only. This is not an official
publication

Motorbooks International books are also available
at discounts in bulk quantity for industrial or sales-
promotional use. For details write to Special Sales
Manager at the Publisher's address

Library of Congress Cataloging-in-Publication Data
Available
ISBN 0-87938-562-6

Printed and bound in Hong Kong

On the front cover: The battleship *Wisconsin* fires
a volley of 16-in. rounds during Desert Storm. *USN*

On the frontispiece: The frigate USS *Brewton* on
patrol in the Persian Gulf. *DoD*

On the back cover: The Persian Gulf Battle Force
was known as Task Force Zulu and included the
carriers *Midway, Roosevelt, America* and *Ranger*.
USN/Rice Inset: Ordnance men transport 1,000-lb.
bombs to an FA-18 aboard the USS *America.*
USN/West

On the title page: Ships of the Red Sea battle
group. Included are the aircraft carriers USS
America, USS *Saratoga* and the USS *John F.
Kennedy. USN*

Contents

In Memoriam

The following is a list of those US Navy personnel who lost their lives during Operation Desert Storm and Operation Desert Shield and to whom this book is respectfully dedicated.

AE3 Michael Belliveau
BT2 Alan H. Benningfield
BTFN Tyrone M. Brooks
AA Christopher B. Brown
AA Darrell K. Brown
AA Steven A. Budizan
AT2 Andrew T. Cady
SN Monray C. Carrington
AN Larry M. Clark
Lt. Patrick K. Connor
Lt. Comdr. Barry T. Cooke
Lt. T. Costen
AMS3 James F. Crockford
AG1 Shirley M. Cross
SM3 Delwin Delgado
Lt. Robert J. Dwyer
AO3 Anthony J. Fleming
Akan Gilbert A. Fontaine
BT3 David A. Gilliland
AEAN Kevin J. Hill
Lt. Daniel V. Hull
BT2 Mark E. Hutchinson
SN Wilton L. Huyghue
Lt. Mark D. Jackson

FC3 Timothy J. Jackson
MMFA Dale W. Jock
AA Alexander Jones
EM3 Daniel M. Jones
AMS2 Troy Josiah
MSSA Nathaniel H. Kemp
Lt. James Love
EM2 Daniel Lupatsky
FN Michael N. Manns, Jr.
AN Brent A. McCreight
BTFA Daniel C. McKinsey
Randy L. Neel
CWO John M. Paddock
BT2 Fred R. Parker, Jr.
AB2 Marvin J. Plummer
DS3 Mathiew J. Schiedler
DK3 Timothy B. Seay
MSSA Jeffrey A. Settini
FTC Jeffrey W. Shukers
MM3 James A. Smith, Jr.
Lt. John M. Snyder
Lt. Comdr. Michael S. Speicher
RMSN Roderick T. Stewart
AM3 Phillip J. Thomas
Lt. Charles J. Turner
BT1 Robert L. Volden
Lt. David A. Warne
AE2 Brian P. Weaver
MS2 Phillip L. Wilkinson

Acknowledgments

The true story of Desert Storm and Desert Shield from both a diplomatic and military standpoint may not actually be known for another twenty-five years, when many of the relevant documents are finally declassified. Until then we will have to make do with what is discernable from those sources that are accessible.

The source I relied on most for excellent and detailed coverage was the *Navy Times*. The articles by David S. Steigman were of exceptional quality. Other articles by John Grady, Tom Philpot, Bill Mathews, Marc Zoltan, John Burlage and others were also excellent.

The daily news coverage of *The New York Times* and the *Virginia Pilot* were important sources. And articles in the US Naval Institute *Proceedings* were helpful, especially those by Dr. Norman Friedman on the Sixth Fleet and the *Vincennes* incident. Thanks also to NAVINT, the international naval newsletter, and editors Desmond Weltern and Antony Preston.

Other publications that I used included *Aviation Week and Space Technology*, *Naval Aviation News* and *Time* magazine.

Television and video sources included Video Ordnance of New York and news reports on Cable News Network (CNN), National Broadcasting Corporation (NBC), American Broadcasting Corporation (ABC) and Columbia Broadcasting Corporation (CBS).

The US Navy provided much source material. Specific thanks are owed to Lt. Comdr. Carrie Hartshorne of CINCLANT Fleet Public Affairs Office for her help on several location shootings. Thanks also to PA1 Chuck Kalnback of the US Coast Guard for both text and pictures of the Coast Guard's activity in Desert Storm and Desert Shield. Many thanks to Ken Carter and Bob Backman for having supplied many pictures.

A special thank-you to the men of the USS. *America* photo lab—Lt. Gary Rice, PH3 Brian Mortimer, PH1 Robert Chouinard, PHAN Derek Walgren, PHAN Jason West, PHC Steven Briggs, PH2 Jeff Smith, PH2 Todd Cichonowicz and PHAN Posnecker—for their very generous photographic contribution to this book.

Other thanks go to Lt. Comdr. Dave Parsons, Bob Dorr, Graham Gaevert of Electric Boat Corp. and George Nanos.

A special thank-you to David S. Steigman for patient guidance, assistance and for also providing much of the information in both of the appendices to this book.

Thanks also to Ellen Gerlitz for her patience and support throughout.

An F-14 lands aboard the USS Eisenhower. *The* Eisenhower *was the second aircraft carrier on the scene after Iraq invaded Kuwait.* Arnold Meisner/ Defense Image

Introduction

When Saddam Hussein invaded the emirate of Kuwait on 2 August 1990 it was the forces of the US Navy that were the first on the scene. The Navy actively supported the international embargo against Iraq and conducted air and surface support actions throughout the active military campaign against Saddam Hussein's war machine. And it will be the Navy that will be on station protecting the United States and coalition interests in the Persian Gulf region long after the majority of the "ground pounders" and "fly boys" have packed their bags and come home. (That is not to say that we won't maintain a ground force and land based air presence in the region for some time.)

This book is the story of the naval campaign in Desert Storm and Desert Shield. This book makes no pretense of being an academic history. Rather, it is what can be called a popular history. It was written, compiled and packaged in a relatively short period of time. It is not footnoted. And most of the source material drawn upon was from contemporary and immediate sources. The book portrays the overall nature of the campaign at sea, but because of its limited space, it was impossible to cover *all* of the actions and operations. Every attempt has been made to be factual, accurate and truthful in the telling of the story of the war at sea. And every attempt has been made to use as much new, exclusive and unpublished photographic material as possible without relying on some of the more spectacular images that have been already widely seen. I hope you enjoy reading it.

Chapter 1

Naval Commitment in the Gulf

On 12 March 1991, the USS *LaSalle* (AGF-3), flagship of the Middle East Task Force, became the first US Navy ship to enter the newly opened port of Ash Shuaybah in recently liberated Kuwait. Although US naval forces are still deployed and on station in Gulf waters, this action with its inherent historic symbolism was one of the final acts of the naval campaign of Operation Desert Storm.

Desert Storm and Desert Shield together may very well be entered into the annals of military and naval history as one of the best engineered, best executed and ultimately most one-sided campaigns of all times. Desert Storm, Desert Shield and the subsequent victory were not accidents or the results of random good fortune, but rather the end product of detailed military planning and the crafting of a consistent and workable foreign policy. State Department Spokeswoman Margaret Tuttweiler stated on 26 March 1991 that "the Department of State was maintaining a consistent foreign policy, even if [we] the press did not think so." This statement came in response to questions over the intent of American policy toward the Saddam Hussein regime in Baghdad during post-cease-fire internal strife in Iraq. This statement

The battleship USS Wisconsin *begins her refit and subsequent return to active service at the Philadelphia Naval Shipyard in April of 1986.* Arnold Meisner/Defense Image

is also a reminder that, as much as a military campaign, Desert Storm has been a foreign policy victory whose success has been every bit as spectacular, though by necessity more low key, than the military campaign. Credit must be given to President Bush's masterful manipulation and balancing of a diverse coalition. It was Clausewitz who in the 19th century postulated that war was the ultimate extension of diplomacy. It might do us well to keep this in mind as we examine the events of Desert Storm and Desert Shield.

We must as citizens of the Global Village try to look at these recent events with some attempt at an informed and hopefully historical perspective—if this is indeed even possible. Some years ago it was firmly maintained that historians had no business looking into the affairs of anything more recent than the Napoleonic Wars. With the passage of time it became acceptable to shine the light of inquiry into events as recent as World War I. Today in what James Burke calls the Age of Information we voracious consumers of information demand instant and expert analysis of events that are still ongoing and evolving right in front of us. The war in Vietnam was termed the dinner-table war because the day's footage was in the studio in time to make that night's evening news, so American families were able to watch the daily war news while they ate their dinner.

Desert Storm happened live during the news. Tom Brokaw interrupted his planned edition of Nightly News to inform his viewers with a bulletin announcing the first US air strikes on 16 January. This was followed almost immediately with the statement that we had the first footage in already, and both he and the network's Pentagon correspondent, Fred Francis, were together unable to correctly identify a US Air Force F-15E Strike Eagle being loaded up with 2,000-lb. bombs. They thought it was an FB-111. "An F-15 can't carry that big an external load," they agreed.

Desert Storm has come to be known as the prime-time war. Thanks to an eight-hour time difference and twenty years of improved video and telecommunications technology, Americans witnessed the war virtually live, and any coverage that was not live was at the speed of instant replay. Data uplink, satellite transmission and the coming of age of the Cable News Network (CNN) have given us a new vision of current events. Nothing that we have seen or experienced on television, with the possible exception of the assassination of President John F. Kennedy and the assassination of Lee Harvey Oswald three days later, have been able to beat the immediacy of a Scud missile attack. National Broadcasting Corporation's (NBC) Arthur Kent and CNN's Charles Jaco have gained national

Pilots preflight their aircraft prior to air operations on 28 January 1986 aboard the USS Saratoga *in the* Mediterranean during air operations against Libya. USN

prominence for reporting back to America live while under attack. American Broadcasting Company's (ABC) reports from Tel Aviv with Martin Fletcher wearing a gas mask were nothing less than bizarre—shades of a midcentury Orwellian nightmare come to life.

Who would have thought two years ago that scenes resembling that of the Blitz in 1940 would become the everyday norm in Tel Aviv, Riyadh and Dhahran? Whole populations were living in 1991 as people did during the days of the Blitz or the V weapons attacks on London. And they were living under the tyranny imposed by the fear of Hussein's weapons—not just the damage that they caused, but rather the fear of the damage that they might cause should even one of

them be equipped with any one of a number of possible chemical or biological warheads. Saddam Hussein had already shown us what he was capable of. The world had no delusion about that!

Even more bizarre was the emergence from the depths of the film archives of the lines of blinded gas victims of World War I: soldiers marching in single file, their faces wrapped in bandages, each man with his left arm on the left shoulder of the man before him.

American military medical experts reviewed long-forgotten papers on the treatment of mustard gas injuries suffered by soldiers in World War I.

During the 1980s the United States built up the base at Diego Garcia as a logistical presence in the Indian Ocean. In this picture the aircraft carrier Saratoga *is moored in the deep water anchorage in 1986.* DoD

13

There are several important differences between the air and land battles of Desert Storm and the naval campaign. Of the three branches of service (Air Force, Army and Navy—the Marine Corps is under the management of the Navy Department) only the Navy has a history of maintaining a presence in the region. *Furthermore, it is this previous history of a naval commitment to the region that validates the stated objectives of Desert Storm.* Certainly the reflagging of the Kuwaiti oil and gas tankers in 1987 indicates and establishes a definite precedence for US military presence in the Persian Gulf region, let alone our specific intentions to maintain Kuwaiti territorial independence. In this

regard the Bush administration's policy can be viewed as merely a continuation of the established policies of the previous Reagan administration.

For a better understanding of US commitment to the region it is necessary to look at the naval operations of the last twelve years. While the scope of this book does not allow for a detailed study of the naval operations during this period, some mention of the details should be given.

The structure and operations of the US Navy has been along two completely diverse but parallel paths for the last decade. The primary consideration in recent naval planning has been

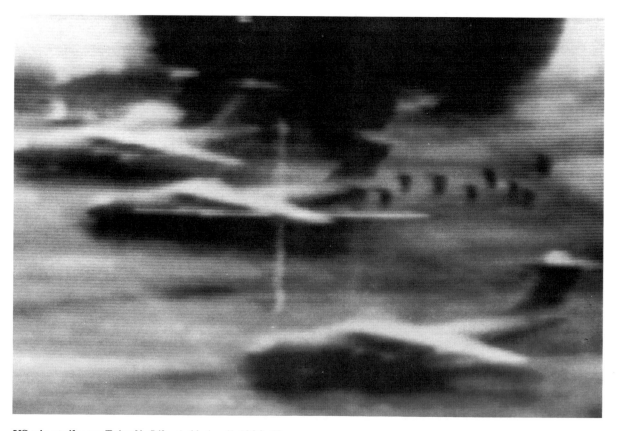

US air strike on Tripoli, Libya, 14 April 1986. The photograph was taken by an FB–111 using the Pave Tack Laser Guided Delivery System. DoD

14

with regard to the US Navy versus the Soviet Union and its ever-growing international naval presence. Modern naval construction and subsequent fleet operational considerations perpetually stress the ever-present Soviet threat and the need for the United States to keep pace with it.

The Navy also needs to fulfill the requirements placed on it by various world commitments that have nothing to do with the Soviet threat. The Navy needs to show the flag, protect US interests abroad, keep the international sea lanes open, protect the rights of US flag carriers and assert the US Navy's right to sail in international waters.

Modern American interest in the Persian Gulf region goes back as far as the late 1940s with the establishment of the Middle East Task

Photograph of damage inflicted by US Navy attack bombers during the 14 April raid on Tripoli, Libya.
DoD

15

Force. At the time it was only a small collection of a few destroyers to represent American interests in the Persian Gulf region. This region was, however, until the early 1970s in the British sphere of influence, and it was the Royal Navy whose ships patrolled these waters. Throughout the 1950s and 1960s visits to the Indian Ocean and Persian Gulf by major fleet elements were infrequent. The *Constellation* visited the Gulf in 1974, and the *Midway* the Indian Ocean in 1977–1978.

Throughout the 1970s and beyond, the United States practiced what was called the twin pillars (Iran and Saudi Arabia) policy to maintain peace and stability in the Persian Gulf region. By relying on the governments of Saudi Arabia and Iran to maintain regional security, the United States could realize its foreign policy goals with only a minimum of direct involvement.

In 1979 the Shah of Iran was deposed and replaced by the hostile fundamentalist Islamic theocracy of the Ayatollah Khomeini. The embassy staff was taken and held hostage for over 400 days, and the US government found itself virtually powerless to act decisively in any way. Every night the new ABC news show "Nightline" reverberated with the theme "America Held Hostage." The United States discovered to its chagrin that it was powerless to act militarily. The rescue attempt by US Air Force (USAF) transport aircraft and helicopters from the USS *Nimitz* with a force under the command of Colonel Beckwith met up with disaster at the Desert One site, and nothing was accomplished. Nevertheless the US Navy was ordered to concentrate its aircraft carrier forces in the area. The extended carrier deployments became known as Gonzo Station, and stressed already hard-pressed morale. It became evident that US ability to project a creditable naval presence was questionable. While it was still possible for the United States to deploy upward of three carrier battle groups in a given area, it was at great expense and seemingly without any direct effect on the political situation. The traditional military institutions were finding it difficult to be effective against the new forms of warfare: state-sponsored terrorism, hostage taking and international blackmail.

Also in 1979 the Soviet Union invaded Afghanistan. This threat to the stability of the region added to the situation in Iran caused the United States to create the Indian Ocean Task Force at that time. This force usually consisted of a carrier battle group composed of ships taken from forces of the Sixth and Seventh fleets, thereby increasing the ability of the US Navy to concentrate naval forces in the region and at shorter notice. From this point on the Persian Gulf and Indian Ocean areas were no longer on the back burner of American foreign policy.

The Rapid Deployment Force (RDF) was created in 1979. Sometimes known as the RJDTF, the RDF eventually evolved into Central Command (CENTCOM), the combined joint service command that would, under the direction of its talented commanding officer Gen. H. Norman Schwarzkopf, carry Desert Shield and Desert Storm to its stunning conclusion. The RDF, bedeviled with structural problems from

The USS Missouri *is pushed into San Francisco Bay in 1986 prior to her recommissioning.* DoD

the start, was short-lived. It had no dedicated forces of its own. Whatever troops were needed to fulfill its designated mission had to be requisitioned from other standing missions such as the defense of Western Europe. What RDF did do was lay the groundwork for the creation of Central Command and recognize the problems and initiate the planning that eventually allowed the United States to respond as quickly and effectively as it did in the early days of Desert Shield. Central Command's specific mission was the reaction to any hostile action threatening the vital interests of the United States in the strategic and volatile Middle East-Persian Gulf region.

The name of the game became the rapid transport, simultaneously by air and sea, of large numbers of troops and their associated supporting supplies and resupplying them adequately once they were established within the theater of operation. The *Algol*-class transports were acquired for use by the United States Naval Service (USNS). These are ships that are owned by the US government but crewed by civilians. These ships are 964 ft. long, have a displacement of 55,000 tons, a speed of 33 knots and were used

Reflagged Kuwaiti tankers in convoy. Here Bridgeton *is seen from the USS* Kidd *in August 1987.* DoD

USS *LaSalle*

On 22 February 1964, twenty-three months after her keel was laid at the New York Naval Shipyard in Brooklyn, New York, the present *LaSalle* was commissioned LPD–3. She joined her sister ships USS *Raleigh* and USS *Vancouver* as the third in a class of new amphibious transports.

As an Amphibious Transport Dock, *LaSalle*'s trademarks were mobility, flexibility and versatility. It has the capability to carry more than 800 combat-ready Marines at high speed to an area of amphibious operations. In addition, it can transport ammunition, cargo, vehicles and fuel to support the Marines.

Within its well deck, which can be flooded, boats are carried to transport men and materiel ashore. The offloading of equipment and supplies is expedited by the use of a deck-mounted crane, elevators and conveyors, plus a six-unit monorail and overhead crane system within the well deck. The flight deck is available for airlifting men and supplies by helicopter.

LaSalle's operating schedule has been anything but routine. In May 1965 she served

The USS LaSalle, *flagship of the Middle East Task Force in her distinctive white scheme.* USN

as flagship for Commander, Amphibious Forces Atlantic during the Dominican Republic crisis. In December of the same year, it helped evacuate Construction Battalion Six from Guantánamo Bay, Cuba, and carried 950 tons of equipment back to the United States.

In November 1966 it made history by being the first ship of its size to successfully recover a *Gemini* capsule and the first ship ever to return a capsule to Cape Canaveral after recovery. In May 1969 it served as an experimental launching platform for Hawker Harrier aircraft.

Through 1971 *LaSalle* served as an amphibious force flagship for various commands. Operating in the Atlantic, Caribbean and Mediterranean areas, it took part in numerous amphibious exercises with US forces in conjunction with other NATO navies.

Selected to replace the USS *Valcour* (AGF–1) as flagship for Commander, Middle East Force (COMIDEASTFOR), in January 1972, *LaSalle* shortly afterward began an extensive overhaul. New facilities were installed to suit her new role. She was outfitted with elaborate command communications equipment, a weather satellite receiver, additional air-conditioning, a modern dental facility, sophisticated closed-circuit television systems, accommodations for an admiral and his staff, a helicopter hangar and a ceremonial awning on her flight deck.

With a coat of white paint to reflect the Middle East's hot sun, LPD–3 became AGF–3 (miscellaneous command ship) on 1 July 1972, and on 24 August *LaSalle* assumed its new duties, reporting to Manama, Bahrain, as a member of the Overseas Homeporting Program. On 30 June 1977 its homeport was changed to Norfolk, Virginia.

Since its designation as COMIDEASTFOR flagship the "Great White Ghost of the Arabian Coast," as *LaSalle* is affectionately called by the crew, steamed an average of 55,000 miles annually, paying call on ports in Africa, Asia and the Middle East. She also participated in annual naval exercises with allied nations in the area.

In February *LaSalle* assisted in the evacuation of 260 American and foreign citizens from the Iranian seaport of Bandar Abbas. The evacuees were shuttled by two British hydrographic ships to *LaSalle*, which was waiting off the Iranian coast.

At the beginning of the Iranian Hostage crisis in November 1979, *LaSalle* was the focal point of US activity in the Persian Gulf. While on station off the coast of Iran, *LaSalle* was at sea from 19 November 1979 to 23 January 1980, a total of seventy-four consecutive days at sea, earning the Navy Unit Commendation pennant.

The combination of the Iranian hostage crisis, and the Iran-Iraq War, which began during the summer of 1980, brought about a dramatic increase in the command and support responsibilities placed upon the crew. For their efforts during those arduous contingency operations, the crew was awarded the Navy Expeditionary Medal.

LaSalle was relieved as flagship for COMIDEASTFOR in November 1980, by the USS *Coronado*. While returning stateside for the first time in over eight-and-one-half years, *LaSalle*'s crew rescued six Norwegian merchant mariners from their burning vessel off the coast of Sardinia.

Shortly after its arrival stateside in December, *LaSalle* began a $60 million overhaul at the Philadelphia Naval Shipyard. Many changes were made to the ship, including a significant increase in the capability of the air-conditioning, replacing and upgrading the ship's four turbine generators, adding a large electronics package, removing two 3-in. anti-aircraft guns, and replacing them with a Phalanx Close-in Weapons System (CIWS). After the completion of the overhaul in August 1981, *LaSalle* returned to the Persian Gulf where it resumed its duties as the flagship for COMIDEASTFOR.

to compete with air freight from the United States and Europe until the drastic increase in the price of oil made their commercial operation unprofitable.

The acquisition of other transport ships for use as a Maritime Prepositioned Force (MPF) and the establishment of a base at Diego Garcia in the Indian Ocean as a base for the MPF were to prove vital in the success of Desert Shield and Desert Storm.

The Sixth Fleet

The Sixth Fleet has since the end of World War II maintained a presence in and watched over the Mediterranean.

In 1981 the Sixth Fleet made it perfectly clear to Colonel Qaddafi that it would not be deterred and would back up with force if necessary its right and intention to patrol international waters. The Line of Death existed only in the mind of Colonel Qaddafi.

Again in April of 1986 it was the Sixth Fleet that revisited Colonel Qaddafi to vent the American government's displeasure with the Colonel for what the United States government regarded as international terrorism directly attributable to the operatives of the Libyan government. This time the US Navy's attack aircraft operated from the carriers *Coral Sea* and *America* along with US Air Force FB-111s flying from the United Kingdom. In a subsequent related action against the Libyan Navy, two Libyan high-speed gunboats were destroyed by the first use of air-launched Harpoon missiles at sea by the US Navy.

In 1982 and 1983 the Sixth Fleet operated in support of US troops deployed in Lebanon. After the bombings of the US Embassy and the Marine barracks, the Sixth Fleet conducted carrier air strikes on positions in the Lebanese Bekaa Valley. The newly recommissioned battleship *New Jersey* fired her 16-in. guns in anger for the first time since the battleships were reactivated. *New Jersey* fired 258 rounds. Additional 5-in. gunfire was also provided by frigates and destroyers of the Fleet. Lebanon also saw the first operational deployment of the Aegis guided missile cruiser. Both the USS *Ticonderoga* and

19

the USS *Yorktown* were deployed with the Sixth Fleet.

In 1985 the Sixth Fleet came into the headlines with its role in the pursuit and capture of the terrorists who had attacked the Italian cruise ship *Achille Lauro*. Clearly the Sixth Fleet was to be used in the area as one of the United States' primary tools in its pursuit of international terrorism.

In August of 1984 a Soviet freighter reported hitting a mine in the Red Sea. The ship reported severe damage but remained afloat. Soon after that there were other reports of contacts with mines and subsequent sightings. The result of this maritime mystery was that the responsibility for the sowing of the minefield was eventually put on a Libyan registered freighter that had passed through the region. It was the newest incident of Libyan complicity in international terrorism.

The subsequent response by the Western powers was to send minesweeping vessels to the region to engage in the elimination of this new menace. The need for new and state-of-the-art minesweeping techniques was to underscore the US Navy's own weakness in this highly specialized field. The burden of the minesweeping work was to fall on the navies of the Western European nations who had developed state-of-the-art techniques.

The Iran-Iraq War

In September of 1980 Saddam Hussein of Iraq attacked the Islamic Republic of Iran,

USS Bunker Hill *(Aegis guided-missile cruiser) during its first deployment in the Persian Gulf.* DoD

ostensibly over control of the Shaat al Arab waterway separating the two countries from each other, this area having been an issue of contention between the two countries for some time. The resultant war engulfed the region for over ten years and saw the US Navy come into conflict with both of the parties involved.

The military regime in Iraq had been conducting a major military force build-up since about 1974 when, with the sudden and massive jump in oil revenues, it increased its military spending drastically.

The first casualties at sea during the Iran-Iraq War were inflicted upon several European tankers during the land battle for the Iranian port of Karumshar early on in the land fighting.

As the war progressed strikes against the Iranian commercial oil terminals at Kharg Island and the Iraqi terminals at Basra illustrated that civilian and commercial targets were of prime importance to both sides. While Iran had a much larger navy than Iraq, there was relatively little surface action between these two belligerents at sea. Along with Iraqi attacks on the oil terminals came Iraqi attacks on the tankers of nonbelligerents doing business with the Iranian government. These attacks on shipping by Iraq, which started in 1981, went unanswered by Iran until 1984.

The Iraqi attacks primarily took the form of French Exocet missiles launched from helicopters. Because helicopters have limited range combat capabilities, it became inevitable that the means for delivering the very deadly missile would escalate. The French-built Super Entendard and Mirage F-1 would become the primary delivery platforms for the Exocet.

In 1984 the Iranians made their first attacks on nonbelligerent commercial tankers sailing out of Iraqi oil ports. Because Iran had more limited access to world weapons suppliers, the equipment available was less sophisticated and less effective. The first air attacks on tankers sailing out of Iraq took the form of American-built F-4 Phantoms firing Soviet-built short-range air-to-surface missiles that were only minimally effective. These attacks were followed by surface attacks involving high-speed

boats manned by Iranian naval personnel and Revolutionary Guards firing lightweight guns and other hand-held weapons such as rocket propelled grenades (RPG) and the like. While these weapons were nowhere near as destructive as the Iraqi-launched Exocets, they were lethal to the crews of the virtually defenseless commercial tankers. As the attacks became more numerous, the European nations increased their naval presence in the region to render support and protection to vessels of their respective flags. Throughout this period there was a continual growth in the degree of commitment to protecting merchant shipping, extending the umbrella of protection to merchant ships whatever their flag.

The capture of the Iran Ajir, *an Iranian ship engaged in mine-laying operations in the Persian Gulf. The ship was boarded and captured on 22 September 1987. A landing craft from the USS* LaSalle, *flagship of the Middle East Force, can be seen alongside. DoD*

Reflagging Kuwaiti Tankers

Meanwhile Iranian speedboat, frigate and mine attacks on shipping out of Iraqi ports increased. The Iranian government further stated its intention to bring the war at sea to the commercial tankers of the other Gulf states that were friendly to Iraq. The threat as stated fell heavily on the merchant fleet of the emirate of Kuwait. It was the decision of the Reagan administration that this situation was intolerable, and its solution was the reflagging and renaming of the Kuwaiti merchant fleet in US colors and registration. Henceforth it was announced that reflagged Kuwaiti tankers would travel through the Persian Gulf to the Strait of Hormuz in convoy under the escort of surface ships of the US Navy. This represents a major historical precedent for the United States, and certainly sets the stage for a direct US involvement in support of Kuwaiti sovereignty and territorial security. While sensational at first these convoys soon settled into an uneventful routine. The United States had made its point.

The *Stark* Incident

On 17 May 1987 the USS *Stark*, an *Oliver Hazard Perry*-class guided-missile frigate, was struck by Iraqi Exocet cruise missiles. While the fires were controlled and the ship was saved, thirty-seven crew members lost their lives in the attack. The *Stark* had not fired on its attacker because the *Stark's* mission was to provide a neutral presence, and to fire on an unidentified aircraft even if it presented a threat would be in violation of the very limited rules of engagement that it was operating under. Furthermore, the length of time in which naval opponents could act or react was so limited by the technologies of modern state-of-the-art weapons that the old adage was to prove true: "He who hesitates is lost." The tragedy of the *Stark* reminded the United States of the dangerous nature of the region even if the intention was peaceful. The *Stark* remained seaworthy and returned to her homeport of Mayport, Florida, under her own steam, a tribute to the survivability of American ships. The Iraqi government claimed that the attack on the *Stark* was accidental, and an American delegation went to Iraq to meet with its military leaders to ensure that this tragedy would never be repeated. The *Stark* tragedy was also proof that there was an urgent need for a reexamination of the existing rules of engagement for US naval forces in the very crowded and dangerous war zone.

Iranian command and control platforms at Rashadat that were destroyed in retaliation for attacks on shipping, 19 October 1987. DoD via Defense Image

Iran Mines the Gulf

In September of 1987 the US Navy attacked and seized the *Iran Ajir*, an Iranian Navy landing craft that had been converted to conduct mine-sowing operations. The ship was captured totally intact and with its cargo of mines, proof positive that Iran was sowing minefields in international waters. As punishment for Iranian actions the *Iran Ajir* was sunk by the detonation of explosive charges placed onboard.

The sinking of the *Iran Ajir* resulted in a period of relative peace at sea that lasted until 14 April 1988 when the USS *Samuel F. Roberts* (FFG-58) steamed into an uncharted minefield off the coast of Bahrain. The *Roberts* was operating in support of US naval forces escorting reflagged Kuwaiti tankers in the Persian Gulf. The *Roberts* suffered extreme structural damage, but thanks to herculean efforts by her crew, the ship was saved. The mine opened up a hole on the port side about 23 ft. by 15 ft., causing damage to both her reduction gear and shaft. Ten crewmembers were injured, some seriously. The mines in the minefield were clearly of Iranian manufacture and dated 1987, proving that the Iranians were back in the mine-sowing business.

The resultant retaliation was given the code name of Operation Praying Mantis and became the largest surface action for the US Navy since World War II. The action took place on 18 April 1988 and was marked by the destruction of the Sirri and Sassan oil platforms in the southern part of the Persian Gulf. The US claimed that the platforms intended for gas and oil separation were in fact being used by Iranian Revolutionary Guards as observation platforms to conduct hostile operations against unarmed merchant ships.

Operation Praying Mantis represented several notable tactical achievements. Praying Mantis was the first combat test of new planning and command structure involving the integration of air and surface elements, intelligence support, communications and new rules of engagement.

The next threat to shipping and general security in the Gulf region came from the construction of missile sites by the Iranians. These missile sites were to accommodate Chinese-built Silkworm surface-to-surface missiles, a weapon that presented a very real danger to interna-

tional shipping in the narrow waters of the Persian Gulf and especially the Strait of Hormuz. If a missile found its mark at the Strait of Hormuz and sank a large supertanker, the entire Persian Gulf could be sealed up for a long time. To counter this potential threat the USS *Vincennes* was detached from the Indian Ocean force and, after some refresher training, sent into the troubled waters of the Persian Gulf on 16 May 1988. It was felt that the *Vincennes* with its extremely sophisticated SPY 1 phased array radar system could deal effectively with the potential threat to shipping posed by the Silkworm missiles.

The *Vincennes* Incident

Much has already been written and in great detail of the tragic events of 3 July 1988, and there is no doubt that some details still remain to be told. Briefly put, the *Vincennes* opened fire with her two 5-in. guns on a number of Iranian

The Iranian frigate Sahand, *hit by Harpoon missiles and laser-guided bombs, is shown on fire after retaliation for damage inflicted on the USS* Samuel Roberts *by a mine.* DoD

speedboats after they opened fire on the *Vincennes*'s SH-60B helicopter. The forward 5-in. gun jammed after only about a minute of firing, leaving only the aft 5-in. gun serviceable. The *Vincennes* still fired about seventy-two rounds, maneuvering wildly and erratically to maintain the aft gun on target, while the USS *Elmer Montgomery* was credited with the destruction of one of the speedboats. Iran Air Flight 655 was detected about two minutes before the surface action began. The aircraft was identified as unknown and presumed hostile. The ship herself was stationed roughly on the boundary of the commercial air lane, with the Iran Air flight 655 headed straight at it. The TIC (tactical information coordinator) read the unknown contact as descending and conveyed this information to the captain and the AAW (anti air warfare) officer. While the AAW officer requested permission to fire at twenty miles' distance, the captain held his fire until the aircraft, which was still thought to be descending, was ten miles out. Two standard missiles were fired and struck the target at about seven miles out. The aircraft crashed into the sea killing all of the 290 persons aboard.

The US naval forces had been warned by the government in Washington of the possibility of Iranian suicide attacks on American ships during the upcoming Fourth of July holiday. That combined with the very graphic memories of the fate of the *Stark* on the mind of the crew of the *Vincennes* led to a crisis mentality that resulted in tragedy. This is only a simplified account of the events as they happened. There were other points of contention, such as transponder discrepancies, inability to obtain visual confirmation of the target prior to opening fire, repeated unsuccessful attempts at radio contact and an inability to establish civilian airline schedule deconfliction.

The heavy death toll of the *Vincennes* incident even by Persian Gulf standards brought about a sort of cessation of hostilities for a while at least. In September of 1989 the fragile peace of the region was interrupted by the death in Lebanon of Marine Colonel Higgins. Higgins, who had been serving with the United Nations Peace Keeping Force in Lebanon, had been taken hostage by Iranian-backed fanatics and eventually killed. His executioners then released television footage of the corpse. American leaders were revolted by this action and threatened immediate retaliation. The carriers *Coral Sea* and *America* were immediately dispatched to the area and told to stand by. *Coral Sea* was on her last deployment and this was a fine way to end an illustrious career. *America*, on station in the Indian Ocean, was ordered immediately to proceed through to the Red Sea and place herself within striking distance. While no strikes were launched, once again the one-two power play of deployed forces in both the Mediterranean and Indian oceans were brought into play as the immediate response to a crisis in the region.

What we have seen over a period of a dozen years is the growth of a pattern of commitment in the region.

After almost a decade of protracted war and agony a cease-fire was agreed to by the participants. The cease-fire worked out through the good auspices of the United Nations, though shaky at first, took hold. The campaign on land wound down as well as what became known as the Tanker War at sea. The final cost for the Tanker War was published in an article by Ronald O'Rourke in the 1989 *Naval Review* issue of the US Naval Institute *Proceedings*: 543 attacks were recorded between 1981 and 1988—322 by Iraq and 221 by Iran.

The war came to a halt with the two sides in positions not very far from those at the time that the war started. Gains by Iraqi forces late in the war pushed Iranian forces back to the original frontiers after Iranian offensives dislodged and pushed back Iraqi forces from the positions of original gains made early in the war. Both sides were exhausted from what had become one of the modern world's longer grudge matches. The Iranians, however, were as a nation more exhausted by the long war than were the Iraqis. The Iranians had suffered hundreds of thousands of dead, while the Iraqi dead were considerably fewer. Saddam Hussein had won support for the war at home by minimizing his casualties.

Saddam Hussein Rearms

For a brief period the region seemed almost at peace, but as we now know this was not to last. Saddam Hussein bought the latest military hardware from nations and private arms dealers that at the time were very happy to sell to him.

Early in 1990 there were rustlings in the wind, so to speak. American and British customs investigators seized shipments of what were described as possible triggers for nuclear explosive devices while in transit between the United States, United Kingdom and their intended destination of Baghdad. Saddam Hussein appeared on television and claimed he already had such devices. Shortly after that, British customs officials seized crates of what they claimed were parts for an enormous, high-tech cannon. The Iraqis claimed that these long steel tubes were nothing more sinister than new parts for an oil pipeline. Very shortly after this incident Dr. Geoffrey Bull, a Canadian living in Brussels and reputed to be one of the world's leading experts on artillery pieces and developer of a concept of super cannons, was shot to death outside his apartment. It was clear to those who cared to look that the storm clouds were brewing.

Iraq Invades Kuwait

To quote a *Navy Times* article, "The crisis began in mid-July when Iraqi President Saddam Hussein publicly accused Kuwait of 'stealing' $2.4 billion of oil from an underground deposit that straddles the border between the two countries. In addition, Hussein demanded that Kuwait stop exceeding its OPEC oil production quotas or face retaliation."

Negotiations between the two countries collapsed on 1 August, and within twenty-four hours local press and diplomatic sources reported that massive numbers of Iraqi troops were crossing the border.

Outnumbered and outgunned, Kuwait's 20,000-man military continued to fight the invasion through midday 2 August.

Within twenty-four hours of his occupation of Kuwait, Saddam Hussein declared Kuwait to be Iraq's nineteenth province and that it has been annexed by Iraq.

For the United States and the other Western nations the question had become not just the demand for the removal of Iraqi troops from Kuwait, but a reaction to the very real threat of an Iraqi invasion of Saudi Arabia as well.

Detail of damage suffered by the USS Stark *in an attack by Iraqi air-launched missiles on 17 May 1987.*

25

An Italian Lupo-class *frigate. The Iraqis had four of these ships built in Italy but were unable to take delivery on them.* Raytheon Corp.

Chapter 2

Desert Shield: 2 August 1990 to 16 January 1991

The US Navy found itself doing some rethinking as to the nature of conflict in the world and their role in a conflict should one break out. Early in 1990 the Naval War College in Newport, Rhode Island, practiced a war game scenario with emphasis on thinking beyond the cold war era. The heart of the scenario was crisis situations, one of which included an Iraqi invasion of Kuwait.

On 2 August 1990 Rear Adm. John B. LaPlante was en route to Camp Lejune, North Carolina, to attend a seminar. He had recently returned to the East Coast after having spent two years in Hawaii. He was looking forward to a change of seasons as opposed to the eternal tropical summer of Hawaii. The admiral would still have to wait another year before seeing the fall foliage.

On 16 August 1990 Admiral LaPlante sailed from Norfolk, Virginia, at the head of possibly the largest amphibious assault force since D-Day: Commander Amphibious Group Two and the Fourth Marine Amphibious Brigade under the command of Maj. Gen. Harry W. Jenkins, Jr. The thirteen amphibious ships under the command of Admiral LaPlante sailed at only a few days' notice, a virtual miracle when you consider for a moment the absolute logistical nightmare involved in preparing thirteen amphibious assault ships for operational departure and for a totally unspecified period of time.

They were, however, not the first to respond to the situation. The closest US warships to the scene were those of the Middle East Task Force, composed of six to eight ships. The flagship *La-Salle*, a cruiser, four frigates and a destroyer were 600 miles southeast of Kuwait protecting shipping lanes and participating in a short notice exercise with forces of the United Arab Emirates. The *Independence* carrier battle group, which in recent days had been brought nearer the scene, was steaming north in the Indian Ocean at top speed, while the *Eisenhower* carrier battle group, which was on deployment in the eastern Mediterranean, made ready while awaiting orders to pass through the Suez Canal.

The Royal Navy's Armilla Patrol had been on the scene and under the command of Commodore Paul Haddocks since 20 August. The Armilla Patrol, consisting of one destroyer, two frigates and a tanker were augmented by three mine countermeasures vessels (MCMs) that were stationed in the eastern Mediterranean and subsequently ordered on to the Gulf.

The first stateside departures were on 7 August when the battleship *Wisconsin* departed along with its attendant battle group. Officially this was classified as a routinely scheduled Mediterranean deployment. Once under way the *Wisconsin* battle group joined the aircraft carrier *Saratoga* battle group, which had gotten under way on 7 August from homeport at Mayport, Florida. The *Saratoga* was scheduled to replace the carrier *Eisenhower* on station in the eastern Mediterranean. En route the *Saratoga* and *Wisconsin* battle groups were joined by a Marine Amphibious Ready Group headed by the USS *Inchon* and four other ships: *Nashville, Whidbey Island, Newport* and *Fairfax County.*

The Middle East Task Force was bolstered by the arrival of the Aegis guided-missile cruiser *Antietam* detached from the *Independence* battle group and sent into the Persian Gulf. The Navy also disclosed without further comment that it had dispatched two nuclear-powered attack submarines to the Gulf region.

Ships prepared to depart even before they returned to port. The amphibious transport dock USS *Trenton* prepared to get under way with three days' notice, having just returned to her home port of Little Creek, Virginia, just down the road from the Norfolk Naval Base. The *Trenton* had just returned from a drug interdiction support mission in the Caribbean. The crew on the *Iwo Jima* was lucky—they had ten days to get ready to put to sea. The sailing schedules were so tight that when the *Iwo Jima* finally sailed from Morehead City, North Carolina, after loading 1,500 Marines (about 300 more than normal), piles of equipment were left pierside because there was just not enough time to load it

Equipment of the 24th Infantry Division (Mech.) is onloaded at Savannah, Georgia. USCG/Kalnback

all. There were over 2,000 persons onboard, including the over 600 sailors.

By 8 September the *Iwo Jima* was transiting the Suez Canal and by the twentieth was on station in the Gulf.

Following its arrival in the Persian Gulf area, Amphibious Group Two began a cycle of training exercises to sharpen the fighting skills of the Navy-Marine Corps team. A series of exercises were designed to practice for landings and to acclimate the troops to the desert environment. From Sea Soldier I, conducted from 29 September to 5 October 1990, to Sea Soldier IV, conducted from 19 January to 2 February 1991, all facets of amphibious operations and tactics were exercised. The name of the exercise, Sea Soldier, was translated from the Arabic phrase *Jundeel al Bahr*, which is what the exercises were known as to the host nation.

The entire *Kennedy* battle group sailed with only four days' notice, having returned from workups and been held close to ready for just such a situation.

Within a few short days the Navy had three carrier battle groups, a surface action group headed by a battleship and an amphibious ready group with assorted other fleet elements all headed for the area, with more to follow. The mobilization had just begun.

Allied Ships

The response was not limited to the deployment of US naval forces alone. British, French, Canadian, Australian, the Netherlands, Spanish, Italian and Argentinian ships were to make this the largest international armada to join forces since World War II.

While the ships of the US Navy are for the most part readily deployable, it was quite a different story for many of the other navies. Many ships had to undergo in rush circumstances modifications and conversions that would normally have taken months or might not even have been attempted.

The three Canadian warships that were dispatched to the Gulf had first to undergo an intensive two-week refit in order to bring them up to snuff for the task ahead. The destroyer

HMCS *Athabaskan* and the destroyer escort HMCS *Terra Nova* had their Limbo Mk 10 ASW mortars removed to make room for a Phalanx CIWS. Other modifications include the addition of 12.7-mm. machine guns, two 40-mm. L/60 Bofors guns and extra chaff launchers. *Terra Nova* was also outfitted with two quadruple Harpoon missile launchers, installed in only five days.

The oiler HMCS *Protector* was outfitted with two Phalanx CIWS, one on the flag deck and one on the hangar, as well as the addition of 12.7-mm. machine guns and two 40-mm. L/60 Bofors guns. The twin 3-in. gun mounting previously removed was reinstated and additional chaff launchers and electronic warfare equipment were also added, making the HMCS *Protector* the only oiler in the Canadian Navy with what has become known in the Canadian Parliament as a "war-fighting capability." In addition, *Protector* also had upgrades in all its communications equipment.

The five CH-124 Sea King helicopters embarked on *Athabaskan* and *Protector* had their antisubmarine warfare (ASW) equipment replaced with ESM gear, specifically Racal's Kestrel, and also the addition of 12.7-mm. machine guns. The ships are also defended by Blowpipe missiles operated by thirty-two members of the 119th Air Defence Battery. The use of members of land-based air-defense units onboard ships was a technique successfully pioneered by the British during the heaviest days of the air attack against their ships during the Falklands War with Argentina a decade earlier, when anti-air units of the British Army of the Rhine (BAOR) were hurriedly transferred from Germany and put onboard the ships of the British expeditionary force.

On 13 August the Australian destroyers HMAS *Adelaide* and HMAS *Darwin* sailed for the Gulf from Sydney, and the replenishment ship HMAS *Success* sailed a day later, all three ships having been made ready to deploy with about eighty hours' notice. All three ships made one final stop off at HMAS Sterling near Perth for final supplies and were finally under way on 22 August.

On 27 August three Spanish frigates (*Santa Maria*, *Descubierra* and *Cazadona*) departed for the Gulf, and the French government dispatched the aircraft carrier *Clemenceau* with an air complement of forty helicopters and the cruiser *Colbert* to join the three frigates that they already had on station.

Also on 27 August the USS *Midway* (CV–44) left Yokosuka, Japan, for a three-day shakedown cruise before sailing for the Gulf. With her were the Aegis guided missile cruisers *Bunker Hill* and *Mobile Bay*, as well as the *Spruance*-class destroyers *Hewitt* and *Fife*. Also deployed from the Pacific was the command ship USS *Blue Ridge* along with Vice Adm. Henry A. Mauz who was to be in overall command of the blockading force that was rapidly taking shape.

The coalition forces continued to grow in size: two frigates and a supply ship from the Netherlands, two minehunters and a mine-countermeasures support ship from Belgium, two frigates and two corvettes from Italy, a frigate from Greece, as well as the corvette *Olfert Fischer* from Denmark and the Norwegian coast

A US Coast Guard boat provides security for USNS Pfc. Dwayne T. Williams *in the Persian Gulf.* USCG/Kalnback

guard ship *Andenes* while the British added the destroyers *Gloucester* and *Cardiff*, the frigates *Brazen* and *London* to replace the destroyer *York*, and the frigates *Battleaxe* and *Jupiter*, which have been with the Armilla Patrol since well before the crisis began. Three additional mine-countermeasures ships and a support ship were sent as well. The international naval presence continued to grow.

Also deployed from the United States were the new mine-countermeasures ship USS *Avenger* and the forty-year-old minesweepers USS *Adroit*, USS *Impervious* and USS *Leader*, all of which were to be transported to the Persian Gulf onboard the Netherlands registered heavy-lift ship *Super Servant 3*, which is under special charter. Lifting the minesweepers to the Gulf will save much wear and tear on what are acknowledged to be, with the exception of the *Avenger*, among the most antiquated of the minesweepers out there. The *Super Servant 3* is the same ship that transported the frigate *Samuel F. Roberts* back to the United States in

1988 after it hit the Iranian mine and suffered severe structural damage.

The MCMVs are partially operated by some sixty of the 6,243 of the first US Navy reservists to be activated. The naval reservists are only the tip of the proverbial iceberg. The bulk of the 50,000 reserves called up will affect the other services even more. The reserve call-up was to underscore President Bush's commitment to liberating Kuwait. "We will pursue our objective with absolute determination," President Bush stated.

Among the other naval reservists called up were 400 personnel assigned to mobile inshore undersea warfare units, which will be used to protect ports, harbors, anchorages and offshore oil platforms in the Persian Gulf. Two hundred eighty personnel were assigned to Military Sealift Command to assist shipping in both the United States and Middle East. The largest naval reserve call-up was for 2,400 Navy medical personnel—doctors, nurses (anesthesiologists are classified as nurses), hospital corpsmen and sup-

The Cleveland *arrives and offloads equipment in Saudi Arabia.* DoD

31

port staff. These medical reservists were needed to fully equip the two Navy hospital ships, the *Mercy* (T-AH-20) and *Comfort* (T-AH-19), that were also dispatched to the Gulf, the medical staffs to join up with the ships at a later date. *Mercy* and *Comfort* were each 1,000-bed floating hospitals with fifty trauma stations, twelve operating rooms, a twenty-bed recovery room, eighty intensive-care beds and sixteen light- and intermediate-care wards.

Since 1976 the president has had the authority to recall as many as 200,000 reservists involuntarily for a period of up to 180 days (a 90-day activation plus a 90-day extension). This activation would be extended to a year as the crisis was to drag on, with the justification that in many instances the reserve troops were just finishing the refresher training programs as their initial activations were expiring.

Also in the initial call-up were about 1,200 Coast Guard personnel, primarily reserve port-security units from Wisconsin and Ohio. Their job would be to ensure port security and perform anti-terrorist activities overseas during the various unloading procedures in Saudi Arabia. Some Coast Guard personnel were supervising the stateside loading operations that were ongoing, while others were already over in the Persian Gulf and Red Sea operating under the command of the Navy, participating in shipping interdiction and boarding operations.

In late September the Navy announced a second round of reserve call-ups. Included in the second round were three reserve SEAL (sea, air and land commandos) teams and three reserve special boat units as well as several special warfare headquarters detachments.

Among the second round call-ups were special warfare, intelligence, construction, sealift and logistical support units.

Coast Guard Raider patrol boat searches a local fishing boat. USCG/Kalnback

Some of the logistical support personnel were headed for the US Navy base in Sigonella, Italy. Normally a fairly laid-back installation, Sigonella found itself operating on a seven-day-a-week, around-the-clock basis in support of Desert Shield. Under normal circumstances Sigonella pumped about 1.8 million gallons of aviation fuel in six months. During August Sigonella pumped 3.2 million gallons alone, and in the first ten days of September the base pumped more than one million gallons. With Air Force transport aircraft streaming through, the base was also a focal point for the shipment of ordnance supplies and mountains of sacks of mail.

The arrival of the reservists would allow overworked and exhausted logistical support personnel a little time off.

Blockade

While the ships steamed their way to the Gulf, President Bush, Secretary of State Baker and Secretary of Defense Cheney traveled extensively, assembling a coalition of nations both Arab and Western. Unifying and validating the sense of mission throughout were the resolutions and good auspices of the United Nations. Resolution 661 barring the shipment of specific goods to and from Iraq and Resolution 665 authorizing the searches of merchant vessels were passed giving authority and setting parameters to what the nations of the coalition were able to do. The United Nations resolution sanctioned the use of minimum force and established an embargo that would be better described as a blockade (a much more warlike term). All merchant shipping to or from Iraq or Kuwait was to be closely monitored and their cargo manifests inspected. If they were found to be carrying any contraband they were to be diverted.

The interception policy started on 17 August bore fruit from the start. The first interception of an Iraqi ship happened a day later on the eighteenth when the cruiser USS *England*, and the frigate USS *Vandergrift* made interceptions of Iraqi merchant ships. The first boarding happened on 4 September 1990 when the destroyer USS *Goldsborough* stopped and boarded an Iraqi merchant ship carrying a cargo of tea. The ship was diverted to the port of Muscat.

According to the 8 October *Navy Times*, between 17 August and 27 September there were more than 1,400 interceptions of merchant shipping by the naval forces of the coalition. Out of this total there were four instances where there were shots fired across the bows of Iraqi merchant ships that would not stop when challenged by the Maritime Interception Force (MIF). US naval forces boarded 110 ships, and fifteen ships were boarded by ships of other navies. As of 11 December the number of interceptions had climbed to 5,000 with over 500 boardings.

The US Maritime Interception Forces, composed of both Navy and Coast Guard personnel, were teamed together as they have been in the

Chairman of the Joint Chiefs of Staff Colin Powell addressing assembled crew members of the battleship Wisconsin *in the Gulf 13–15 September 1990.* DoD/Allen

Caribbean on drug interdiction missions. The Coast Guard, part of Law Enforcement Detachments (LEDET), has the experience in boarding and searching ships and knows its way around the cargo manifests and declarations. The Coast Guard had ten LEDET teams operating in Desert Shield: five with naval units in the Persian Gulf and five with ships in the Red Sea.

The entire interdiction operation in the Persian Gulf, Gulf of Oman, Arabian Sea, Indian Ocean and Red Sea is controlled from the flagship of the Middle East Force, the USS *LaSalle*. Besides their interdiction duties, all of the ships provide information back to the *LaSalle*, which acts as a central clearinghouse for data on merchant shipping in the area. Once a month representatives of the fourteen nations participating in the blockade will meet to divide up their respective areas of responsibility. All of the operations are being conducted in strict adherence to the terms and specifications of the United Nations resolution.

The most remarkable aspect of this operation is the fact that all of the maritime interdiction operation is based on nothing more formal than a handshake.

Sea Lift

Although the first troops and equipment poured into Saudi Arabia by air, in the long run ninety-five percent of the war supplies bound for Saudi Arabia would be sent by sea, this according to Air Force Gen. Hansford T. Johnson, commander-in-chief of Transportation Command.

USNS *Antares*

USNS *Antares* is one of eight former SL-7 class ships acquired by the Military Sealift Command (MSC). Fast sealift ships are named after bright stars. *Antares* is one of the twenty brightest stars in the sky and is part of the constellation Scorpio.

The 946 ft. long *Antares* and other SL-7 class ships are among the world's largest and fastest vessels. The Navy uses them to move military equipment—primarily helicopters, tanks and other heavy machinery and vehicles—to support the deployment of military forces worldwide. The ships make up the Fast Sealift Ship program aimed at increasing the mobility and responsiveness of American sealift capability.

This high-speed ship is berthed at Jacksonville, Florida, and is maintained on a four-day ready-for-sea status. This permits rapid delivery of equipment and supplies from the United States to Europe, Southwest Asia or other areas of the world if required. The eight Fast Sealift Ships are capable of carrying the equipment requirements of a heavy armored division.

Antares was delivered to the Navy in July 1984. Formerly a commercial container ship, *Antares* underwent a partial conversion to partial roll-on, roll-off configuration to make the ship more suited to military use. The cargo hold was redesigned into a series of decks connected by ramps so that cargo can now be driven in and out of the cargo area for rapid loading and unloading. Side ports and cranes were added, enabling the ship to handle cargo more effectively.

While in its normal reduced operating status a nucleus crew of nine persons maintain the ship. During activation this crew is augmented by an additional thirty-three crew members. The Fast Sealift Ships are contract operated and crewed by Merchant Marine personnel.

The ships were originally intended to transport transatlantic freight competitively with the airlines. The fuel crisis of the 1970s made the operation of these ships unprofitable, and they were subsequently laid up until their purchase by the US government for conversion to military transports.

They have been used actively on exercise deployments to Europe on Reforger, Egypt for Bright Star, and Korea for Team Spirit exercises.

At the same time that the world's navies were steaming at flank speed to the Indian Ocean, Red Sea and Persian Gulf waters a second drama at sea was unfolding. For years there had been much written about the sad state of American merchant shipping and its woeful inability to fulfill the potential military demands on it in time of crisis.

At its height during World War II the US merchant fleet numbered over 5,000 ships. Since then the number has continually dropped. According to the Navy today there are about 310 civilian-owned ships that are useful for the transport of military loads. The last commercial ship built in the United States was completed in 1987, and only one has been ordered since then.

The crisis in the US Merchant Marine is not just in ships but also in qualified personnel. The number of qualified seamen has declined from about 60,000 during World War II to about 27,000 today. Their average ages today are between forty-five and fifty years of age, with some merchant crew ranging in age up to sixty and even seventy years old. In its search for crews the Department of Defense sought the help of the seamen's unions, which began a telephone search for retired merchant seamen, especially chief engineers and radio operators who were willing to sign on one more time.

With the decline in flag merchant fleet, the US government began to buy retired merchant ships on the international market over the last ten years and place them in the Ready Reserve. Over the last five years the government has spent some $7 billion creating a Ready Reserve fleet of 96 ships. The ships are maintained by the Department of Transportation and are supposed to be ready for real world deployment in five, ten or twenty days.

The Military Sealift Command (which is part of Transportation Command) has so far activated forty of the ninety-six ships in the Ready Reserve, but actually getting them ready to sail has been another story. Some of the ships in the Ready Reserve fleet have not been moved in a decade and consequently would need substantial repairs to make them seaworthy. The activated ships include seventeen roll-on, roll-off ships, thirteen cargo ships, five barge ships, two aviation logistics supply ships and two crane ships to expedite the unloading of containerized cargo on ships without their own cranes. The ships are maintained by the Maritime Administration (MarAd), part of the Department of Transportation, until activated, when they become the responsibility of the Military Sealift Command.

MarAd has a budget of about $750,000 per ship for annual maintenance. Of the forty-six ships activated for deployment in Desert Shield, twenty-six did not meet their reactivation timetables. A number of delays were due to things like faulty pipes, pumps, valves, boilers and other equipment, all of which needed to be repaired before the ships could get under way.

The first supplies to arrive in Saudi Arabia by sea were from the Maritime Prepositioned Force based in Diego Garcia in the Indian Ocean, and the eight fast sealift ships operating as USNS (United States Naval Service) ships. The fast sealift ships are 945 ft. behemoths displacing 55,000 tons and capable of sustained speeds of up to thirty-three knots. They are capable of transporting much of a division's mobility and firepower in one load. They are generally home-ported in seaports around the United States and ready to sail on four days' notice.

The sealift was not without problems. The fast sealift ship *Antares* (T-AKR-294) loaded down with equipment of the 24th Infantry Division (Mech.) suffered boiler breakdowns shortly after leaving Savannah, Georgia. While repairs were effected, continued breakdowns forced the Navy to have to send out a tug to tow her over to Saudi Arabia. While the equipment she carried got there weeks late, it got there nevertheless.

Additional problems occurred with added cargo requirements. The Army's requirement for the 24th Infantry Division stated that it could be moved in seven shiploads, but when it came time to transport the equipment there was 350,000 cu. ft. of additional equipment. Military Sealift Command had to call up an extra Ready Reserve ship and charter a roll-on, roll-off ship to accommodate all the extra gear.

At many ports on all the coasts of the United States the scene was repeated. Long convoys of vehicles traveled from their storage areas and assembly points to the site of the loadout activity. At Savannah, Georgia, where the 24th Infantry Division vehicles and armor were loaded onto ships like the fast sealift ship USNS *Algol* (T-AKR-287). Active duty and reserve personnel from all the services worked side by side around the clock to get the equipment loaded and loaded right. Explosive loading specialists from the reserve units and Maritime Safety Office in Savannah, Georgia, were on hand to ensure that all explosives and vehicles with fuel were properly secured onboard the ships. Active duty port security units, including the Coast Guard Patrol Boat group from Key Largo, Florida, provided around-the-clock port security.

The thirteen Maritime Prepositioning Ships (MPS) are slightly smaller than the fast sealift ships, displacing 40,000 to 48,000 tons fully loaded, and measuring anywhere from 673 to 821 ft. in length.

Organized into three squadrons, four ships are berthed at Atlantic ports, four ships at Guam and five at Diego Garcia. Each squadron carries enough supplies to sustain a Marine Expeditionary Force of 17,000 personnel for thirty days. The ships began unloading their cargoes in Saudi Arabia on 16 August.

There are ten Afloat Prepositioning Force Ships (APFS) that are normally berthed at Diego Garcia. They are kept fully loaded with supplies and are intended to reinforce Army and Air Force units. These ships include two tankers, four container ships, two cargo ships and one float-on, float-off cargo ship. One ship, the *Noble Star*, is a fleet hospital cargo ship capable of off-loading an entire hospital facility onshore. Another APF ship is normally stationed in the Mediterranean.

To help cope with the needs of Desert Shield, Military Sealift Command chartered

USS America *during air ops in the Mediterranean.* USN/Rice thirty-six civilian ships: nineteen US ships and seventeen foreign ships. The ships, all roll-on, roll-off types, would be used for transporting additional supplies from the United States and transporting US units stationed in Europe.

The deployments and sealift needs of Desert Shield forced the Bush administration to reconsider its plan to cancel $212 million in subsidies for US merchant shipping. In 1989 the Commission on Merchant Marine and Defense recommended spending $13 million over a period of eleven years to build up to 194 new ships and buy fifty more, all for possible military use. The commission's recommendations were shelved by the administration, which said that the financing of the proposal was impossible due to budget restraints.

While there has never been a formal treaty between Saudi Arabia and the United States to defend Saudi territory, there has been a special understanding in effect since 1974. The Joint Commission on Security Cooperation between the United States and Saudi Arabia paved the way for a massive build-up of Saudi air, land and sea forces, and a building and development program was put in place to build the massive infrastructure needed to support a major deployment.

Sailors aboard USS John F. Kennedy. *USN*

A total of $17 billion was spent solely on infrastructure through agreements with the Army Corps of Engineers from 1972-1988. The Saudis spent $3.8 billion on the construction of naval facilities alone. In addition to bases and headquarters, the Saudis built a port at Ras al Mish'Ab.

The largest force of Coast Guard personnel serving in the Persian Gulf were the more than 300 reservists that were called to active duty to provide port security to three ports in the Middle East. PSU 301 from Buffalo, New York, PSU 302 from Cleveland, Ohio, and PSU 303 from Milwaukee, Wisconsin, provided around-the-clock security in their 22-ft. Raider patrol boats. Boats that were intended for use on the fresh waters of the Great Lakes were transported to the far-off Persian Gulf and put to service protecting the security zones.

With the help of Saudi Frontier Forces personnel, who were carried on the patrol boats and acted as interpreters, the Coast Guard stopped fishing boats and whatever small craft entered the security zones.

While the Navy's base in Sigonella, Italy, was picking up the logistical slack in the Mediterranean, the Navy's only shore-based facility in the Gulf—the Naval Station at Bahrain—was doing yeoman service to support the ships at sea in the Gulf. Once a very low-key operation, it now became a logistical linchpin in the Navy's resupply operations. Called "the biggest little American base in the world" by Sam Zackheim, the US ambassador to Bahrain, the Bahrain Naval Station was responsible for getting everything from food, ammunition, spare parts, fuel and mail out to the ships and serving also as the only available liberty port for rest and recreation for sailors who had already been at sea for months.

As the situation stabilized—in that no *immediate* military action would be taken—the *Eisenhower* carrier battle group, which had left its homeport of Norfolk, Virginia, on 8 March 1990, was allowed to return home. *Ike*'s tour had been extended by ten days, and its timely response to the Iraqi aggression had been instrumental in ensuring that Saddam Hussein went no further than his invasion of Kuwait. However, the Navy was very sensitive to the stresses placed on the carrier battle groups during the deployments on Gonzo Station during the Iran hostage crisis of a decade earlier, so it now sought to bring the carrier battle group back as close to the six-month deployment schedule as possible.

Ike in the eastern Mediterranean was supposed to have been relieved by the *Saratoga* out of Mayport, Florida. *Sara*, however, was deployed to the Indian Ocean and Persian Gulf instead. In turn *Ike* was relieved on station by the *Kennedy* carrier battle group. The *Kennedy* battle group in turn had been assembled and deployed on four days' notice.

Independence Enters the Gulf

On 2-4 October the *Independence* became the first US aircraft carrier to enter the very narrow confines of the Persian Gulf since the *Constellation* visited the Gulf in 1974. This controversial move seemed to be in total contradiction to existing US Navy policy. The Persian Gulf was not the ideal place for carrier operations. However, if there was to be a military response against Iraq or Iraqi positions in Kuwait it would be necessary to get much closer. Stationed at the entrance to the Gulf the *Indy* was about 1,200 flying miles from any potential target. With the maximum range of Intruders at 900 miles and the maximum range of F-14's at 700 miles, it was necessary to refuel these aircraft at least two times in the course of any combat mission, which put additional strain on an already well-stressed line of supply, as well as decrease the potential offensive capabilities of the air wing. *Indy* set an important example, which showed its worth in the upcoming months.

While in the Gulf *Independence* was to operate in support of operation Imminent Thunder, an amphibious landing exercise on the coast of Saudi Arabia was to give Saddam Hussein cause to wonder and worry. The exercise held from 15 to 21 November was the largest and most ambitious exercise to date. While severe weather caused the cancellation of part of the amphibious operation, enough of the operation went off on schedule so as to prove the feasibility of Persian Gulf operations.

Despite some criticism against deploying *Independence* in the narrow Gulf waters, it was decided that there was more to gain by it operating there despite the potential threat from attack. Critics said that the Gulf was too narrow and crowded to conduct sustained air operations and that in the narrow Gulf the *Independence* presented an almost irresistible target to hostile forces.

The Navy, however, felt that the *Indy* could take care of itself. In the face of a real threat it was capable of launching thirty aircraft in succession with a sixty-second interval between each launch. Furthermore the carrier is capable of firing defensive missiles, chaff and other decoys, and has electronic countermeasures.

The nuclear-powered *Los Angeles*-class attack submarine *Pittsburgh* (SSN–720) was made ready for deployment in seven weeks. On 8 November it departed its base at Groton, Con-

Live fire of a NATO Seasparrow missile on USS America. USN/West

necticut, for the Mediterranean after her crew helped perform the almost impossible. Backed by a pledge of whatever assistance they wanted and whatever resource they needed, the crew of the *Pittsburgh* got the ship through a four-week upkeep, a scheduled seven-week restricted availability, a dry-docking and a ship's battery change. All of this was accomplished in thirty-eight days.

Pierside the farewell scenes were repeated as they had been countless times before, but this time things were a bit different. Instead of a return date there was nothing but a large question mark. Anxious wives, husbands, parents and children wished their loved ones well as they sailed off into uncertainty, leaving family members stateside to cope with life as best they could. By the middle of November the six-month deployment schedule would be scrapped by the chief of naval operations. The ships on deployment then would be there for the duration.

On 30 October at 0815 Bahrain time,

An SH–3 helicopter passes the Rock of Gibraltar. USN/ Rice

tragedy struck the US Navy in the Persian Gulf. Ten sailors onboard the amphibious assault ship USS *Iwo Jima* were killed when a steam valve

USS Ranger *refueled at sea by the USNS* Passumpsic, *which is also providing fuel to the French destroyer* Latouche-Treville *while under way during Desert Shield.* DoD

ruptured in the ship's boiler room. The ship was commissioned in August 1961, and is the Navy's oldest amphibious warship. In recent years it has put in much sea time. Since 1987 it has been on three long-term major deployments and in the last year spent only fifty-six days in port.

Iwo Jima had just departed Bahrain after a port call for repairs and maintenance of various systems including her boilers. After the accident the ship's engines were shut down as a precaution, and it was towed back to Bahrain for additional repairs.

Adm. John LaPlante was put in charge of the preliminary investigation. Subsequent inquiry centered around what were believed to be faulty brass bolts that were installed instead of steel bolts by a civilian contractor hired to perform the work in Bahrain.

While the troops and sailors dug in and stood on station the scene of activity shifted stateside. By the end of November President Bush announced a major shift in US policy. The United States was to send another 200,000 troops to the Gulf plus naval elements that would include three more aircraft carrier battle groups. All of these forces were to be in position by the year's end. This change in policy, and indeed in the overall strategy, was to shift from the defensive protection of Saudi Arabia and its oil fields to a level of force that could and would take the offensive against Iraq. The decision to increase force strength and thus change the stated posture of commitment was followed by congressional hearings to examine US military options in the Gulf.

The hearings scheduled included House and Senate Armed Services Committees, the Senate Foreign Relations Committee and the House Foreign Affairs Committee. The hearings began on 27 November and included a wide range of administration policymakers and influential policymakers of former administrations as well as Middle East and military experts and analysts.

The major issue for consideration was whether the sanctions and quarantine against Iraq were effective, whether or not they should be continued and if so for how long. Witnesses included Secretary of Defense Cheney, Chairman of the Joint Chiefs of Staff (JCS) Gen. Colin Powell, former Chairman of the JCS Adm. William Crowe (Ret.) and former Secretary of State Henry Kissinger.

On 8 December the carrier USS *Ranger* sailed from its San Diego, California, homeport. *Ranger* was followed on 28 December by the carriers USS *America* and the USS *Theodore Roosevelt*, both sailing out of Norfolk, Virginia, on the Atlantic. In addition it was decided to send the battleship USS *Missouri* to join its sister ship, *Wisconsin*, on station in the Gulf. The nine 16-in. guns on each of the battlewagons would prove invaluable in support of any amphibious operation.

While the three carrier battle groups sailed, the *Independence* returned. *Indy* had been deployed since June, a good two months prior to the beginning of the crisis, and had been on station since the crisis began. *Independence* and her escorts would be home for Christmas.

Meanwhile tragedy again struck US naval forces in the Middle East. At 2355 (local time) on 21 December the ferry *Ein Tuvia* carrying 102 sailors from the carrier *Saratoga* capsized and sank in Haifa harbor. Twenty-one of *Sara's* crew drowned. *Saratoga* had put into Haifa on a port call that was supposed to give crew members a well-deserved and much-needed chance for a little shore leave and some R and R in a friendly country.

As the year came to an end the politicians and diplomats continued to talk. Debate at home sharpened; diplomatic negotiations went around in circles getting nowhere until they finally collapsed entirely. In the desert the troops practiced going on the offensive and at sea the pilots sharpened their skills while the ships steamed on.

At the United Nations a new ultimatum gave Saddam Hussein until 16 January to completely withdraw his forces unconditionally and unilaterally from Kuwait. The stage was set for the next act in the drama to begin.

An A–7E Corsair II from the Kennedy. USN/Parsons

Chapter 3

War: The First 48 Hours

The new year began with the convening of the 102nd Congress. Said Speaker of the House of Representatives Thomas Foley, "There's no question that there will be a debate on the question on the use of force in the Gulf."

Congressional debate on the war issue was, however, postponed for more than a week pending the outcome of negotiations in Geneva, Switzerland, between Secretary of State James Baker and the Iraqi Foreign Minister Tariq Aziz. On 10 January the Baker-Aziz talks failed. Said Secretary of State Baker, "Regrettably, I heard nothing today that suggested to me any Iraqi flexibility . . . The choice is Iraq's. If it should choose to continue its brutal occupation of Kuwait, Iraq will be choosing a military confrontation which it cannot win."

In Baghdad, Saddam Hussein threatened that American forces would "swim in their own blood."

On 11 January the congressional debate began. In a uniquely American display of soul-searching, senators and members of Congress of both parties gave impassioned speeches spanning both sides of the war issue. Said Senate Majority Leader George Mitchel (Democrat) from Maine, "It may become necessary to use force to expel Iraq from Kuwait, but because war is such a grave undertaking, with such grave consequences, we must make certain that war is employed only as a last resort."

Speaking in what was a dissenting view was Minnesota freshman Sen. Paul D. Wellstone (Democrat) who said in his first appearance before the Senate, "We must stay the course with economic sanctions, continue the pressure, continue the squeeze, move forward on the diplomatic front, and Mr. President, we must not, must not rush to war."

Speaking for what was to be the majority viewpoint was House Minority Leader Representative Robert H. Michel who said, "Either we stop him now, and stop him permanently, or we won't

General Schwarzkopf and General Waller in their operational command center in Riyadh. DoD

A Tomahawk cruise missile is launched from the USS Mississippi *during Desert Storm.* USN

stop him at all." In the end the Bush administration won the day. The policy of the administration was approved and the legislative decks were cleared for what lay ahead.

As time ran out the last-ditch attempts at conciliation by the United Nations Secretary General Javier Peres de Cuellar came to naught, and the French government ceased to continue its attempts at a negotiated settlement.

In the United States, security was beefed up throughout the country in anticipation of increased terrorist activity. Naval installations such as the naval bases at Norfolk and San Diego greatly intensified security. Civil airports throughout the country took added precautions as well.

In the Gulf the military build-up continued. On 15 January the aircraft carrier USS *America* transitted through the Suez Canal. In two days' steaming it would be within range of Iraqi targets.

The crew of the aircraft carrier *Theodore Roosevelt* would have to wait a little longer. The *Roosevelt*, which left the Norfolk Naval Base on 28 December, would not be in position until some time after the hostilities commenced. The Navy decided that the *Roosevelt* would for the moment be held in reserve to relieve one of the other carriers should that become necessary.

For the crews onboard the Navy ships on station the atmosphere was electric. This was, after all, exactly what they had been training for. The day had come when the red-shirted ammunition handlers onboard the carriers would be wheeling out live ordnance. The pilots in the ready rooms went over their flight plans one more time. It was no secret—for some days now the outlines of the joint air war operations plan had appeared in print in one form or another. The general consensus seemed to be that they were glad to begin fighting because the sooner they pushed the Iraqis out of Kuwait, the sooner they would get back home.

Tomahawks Away

As the deadline came and went nothing happened—for the first twenty-four hours at least. President Bush announced that the Iraqi war machine was operating on borrowed time.

When the war did come at approximately 0300 local Baghdad time, it ushered in a new age in the annals of warfare. The sea war for the liberation of Kuwait opened with a wave of dozens of Tomahawk cruise missiles launched in total darkness by the ships of the US Navy stationed in the Persian Gulf off the coast of Iraq.

The honor of being the first ship to fire a Tomahawk cruise missile goes to the Aegis guided-missile cruiser *San Jacinto*. The *San Jacinto*, which deployed with the *Kennedy* battle group on 15 August, became the first Aegis cruiser to deploy with a full load of 122 Tomahawk cruise missiles. In this configuration the *San Jacinto* is classified by the Navy as a Special Weapons Platform. In effect it became

The Tomahawk launch console on the Aegis guided-missile cruiser Mobile Bay. *The Aegis guided-missile cruiser turned out to be a spectacular launch plat-* *form for the Tomahawk.* Arnold Meisner/Defense Image

Tomahawk Cruise Missile

The circuit ignites a rocket motor that pushes the missile about 200 ft. clear of the ship. During this time wing and tail control fins pop out of the missile, the rocket motor is jettisoned and a jet engine starts to power the missile.

After entering flight an inertial guidance system steers the Tomahawk toward land where its terrain counter-matching system (TERCOM) takes over guidance duties, comparing the ground beneath it with an onboard computer picture of the course that it should be following. TERCOM adjusts the missile's course so the two pictures coincide.

The picture in TERCOM's brain is large enough so that any battle damage sustained by objects in the missile's path won't throw it off course.

Closer to the target, several digital scene-matching correlation updates or DISMACs are made to ensure final run in to the target. The DISMAC ensures that the missile will not get confused on the way to the target, and that it will go after the target even if the target has already been obliterated by prior attacks.

The missile is also equipped with a strobe unit that takes periodic glimpses of the terrain during nighttime operations.

During the Desert Storm operation the Tomahawk scored an impressive ninety-eight percent rate of successful launch and an eighty percent success rate on target.

One of the highlights of CNN's Gulf War coverage was the Tomahawk cruise missile attack that they recorded. The missiles came into downtown Baghdad, turning right and left and on and on almost as if they were following a street map, which is in fact just what they were doing.

The Tomahawk can carry two types of warheads: a 1,000–lb. high-explosive warhead or a warhead that contains about 675 cluster bomblets. Another version of the Tomahawk is capable of carrying a nuclear warhead—naturally, none of these were used in the Gulf war.

A submarine-launched Tomahawk cruise missile. USN

the realization of the Strike Cruiser—a concept proposed in the 1970s and subsequently canceled by the Ford administration.

According to reports, the Aegis guided-missile cruisers *Anteitam* and *Philippine Sea* were also carrying an increased loadout of Tomahawk cruise missiles.

The missiles are stored vertically in two banks of sixty-one launching cells, one forward and one aft. The Mk. 41 Verticle Launch System (VLS) represents the state of the art in launching systems.

Among the ships capable of launching Tomahawks in the Persian Gulf were the battle-ship *Wisconsin*, the Aegis guided-missile cruiser *Anteitam* and the destroyer *David R. Ray*, which between them were carrying an estimated 100 Tomahawks.

Deployed in the Red Sea were the *San Jacinto, Philippine Sea* and the *Spruance*, which between them had an estimated 191 Tomahawks onboard. The *Midway* battle group just entering the Persian Gulf had an estimated fifty-seven Tomahawks with it. In addition the *Los Angeles*-class attack submarines *Louisville* and *Pittsburgh* were deployed in the Red Sea and Persian Gulf, respectively, and were subsequently the first submarines to ever launch

As the air war begins, 1,000–lb. bombs are transported to waiting A–6 Intruder aboard the USS America. USN/West

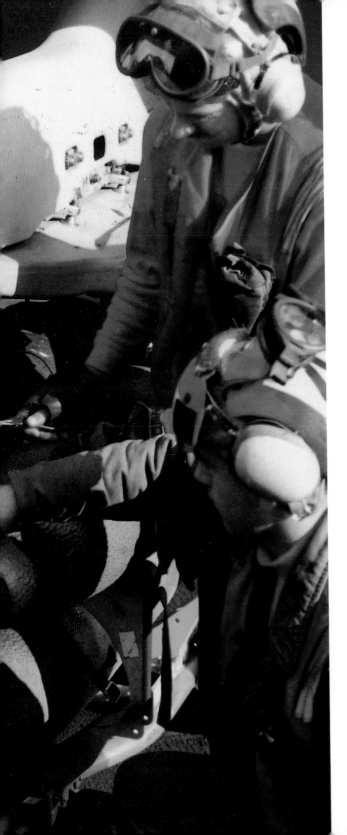

Tomahawks in combat. While all the subs of the *Los Angeles* class are capable of launching Tomahawks, both the *Louisville* and the *Pittsburgh* are early improved models of the class and have six twin-Tomahawk launch cells located in their bows.

While *San Jacinto* has the credit of launching the first Tomahawk, the battleship *Wisconsin* was certainly the most visible launch platform. When the video and stills of the Tomahawk strikes were broadcast and printed in the newsmagazines it was the *Wisconsin* that received the lion's share of the publicity.

The *Wisconsin* sailed from Bahrain on 13 January to get into position for the commencement of hostilities on the seventeenth. In addition to launching its own Tomahawk missiles the *Wisconsin* acted as Tomahawk Strike Warfare Commander for the Persian Gulf, coordinating the launch sequence of Tomahawks during the initiation of hostilities.

The *Wisconsin* launched eight of her thirty-two Tomahawks in the first volley of forty-seven Tomahawks launched from the Persian Gulf in the early hours of action on 17 January. On *Wisconsin* the Tomahawks are launched from eight armored box launchers, each of which contains four Tomahawks.

The Navy claims that of the first fifty-one missiles launched on 17 January fifty hit their target, and one failed to achieve successful launch. This is somewhat better than the eighty-percent average achieved during the war.

In Baghdad at 0300 on 17 January the first cruise missile barrage hit home with devastating accuracy, destroying much of the Iraqi military's first-line command, control and communications capability. Direct hits by cruise missiles were reported on the Defense Ministry and the Baghdad Telecommunications Center.

Amazing videos of these first attacks on Baghdad were broadcast virtually live by both Bernard Shaw and Peter Arnett of CNN broad-

Red-shirted ordnance men adjust the fuses on Mk. 82 500-lb. bombs onboard the aircraft carrier USS America. *USN/West*

53

casting from their hotel room in the Hotel al Rashied, which was to become famous as the international press headquarters in the upcoming weeks. The fact that the press could operate this close to the scene of action without being in any real danger says much for the ability of the US armed services to put ordnance on target with exact precision.

Until 17 January the capabilities of the Tomahawk were only theoretical, with its reputation based solely on test results.

The Navy's interest in the Tomahawk started in the late 1970s with the nuclear-armed version of the Tomahawk as a practical and cheap way around the limitations of the Strategic Arms Limitation Treaty (SALT) II on US nuclear warheads. The Navy only began to take delivery of the land-attack version of the Tomahawk in March of 1986, and reportedly had in its possession an inventory of only about 1,000 of them.

First Carrier Strikes

As the ordnance handlers on the aircraft carrier *John F. Kennedy* moved cluster bombs and high-explosive bombs into place, the carrier

Ordnance men load a Sidewinder missile onto an F-14 of VF-33 during Operation Desert Storm. USN/ Briggs

bustled with activity in preparation for an 0120 aircraft launch. Between 0110 and 0600 the *Kennedy* launched forty-one aircraft, thirty-three in the first wave. The first four aircraft were F-14s that flew the dawn sweep to make sure that there was airborne no Iraqi opposition. They were followed by four more F-14s in the HVU (High Value Unit). Their task was to escort the attack aircraft armed with HARM missiles. Then came the attackers: two A-7 Corsair IIs armed with TALD (Tactical Air Launch Decoy), sixteen A-7s armed with HARMS, six A-6E Intruders armed with LGBs (Laser Guided Bombs) and three EA-6E Prowlers armed with

HARMS. They in turn were followed by one E-2C Hawkeye, one KA-6D tanker and two A-6Es armed with both HARM and TALD weapons. The *Kennedy* also launched two SH-3 Sea King helicopters flying as plane guard to fish anyone out of the drink if they had to bail out. The final launch was two S-3 Viking aircraft at 0600, flying as air refuelers.

The TALD made its operational debut in the Gulf war and proved itself extremely effective. Manufactured by Brunswick Defense of Stoke, Illinois they were used with exceptional effectiveness during the first three days of the air war on air defense suppression missions. Their role

Even the forces at sea had to be prepared for the possibility of chemical attack. ABFN Franklin

Grahm fuels an F-14A while wearing an MCU-2P gas mask on USS Kennedy. *DoD*

During the initial phase of the Desert Storm, US Navy aircraft flew into land bases before they began their strikes into Iraq and Kuwait. This enabled them to carry a maximum bomb load and allowed the aircrews to benefit from the maximum coordination of joint operations. USN

The low-level view from the cockpit of an A-7E from the aircraft carrier John F. Kennedy. USN/Leenhouts

A–7E Corsair II from the USS John F. Kennedy *during Desert Storm.* USN/Parsons

An EA–6B Prowler in action during Desert Storm. It was reported that every time a Prowler went in with attacking aircraft the Prowlers were 100 percent effective in neutralizing antiaircraft radars and missile sites. USN/Parsons

is to entice enemy radars to turn on, thus exposing the radars to attack and destruction by HARM missiles. The TALDS were also used to "soak up" Iraqi surface to air missiles, a very cost effective tradeoff.

From the first strike, the air war at sea was complicated by the fact that there was no direct data link between the Air Force air-war controller on the ground in Riyadh and the carriers at sea, which meant that the ATO (Air Tasking Order), a 900-page document detailing all the specifics of the air operations, had to be manually transported on a computer hard disk from the Air Force headquarters in Riyadh to the battle force commanders at sea, and from there by helicopter to each of the individual carriers. Every morning at 0200 a pilot from the *Kennedy* in the Red Sea and the *Theodore Roosevelt* in the Persian Gulf flew an S-3 Viking from the ship to Riyadh to pick up the ATO package and fly it back to the ship. Once on the ship, the air crews found their missions on the ATO and prepared for the day's attacks. It was possible to make corrections and alterations to the ATOs via the satellite hookup with Riyadh.

Instead of flying directly to target locations, some of the *Kennedy*'s aircraft first flew into air force bases in Saudi Arabia to refuel before flying on to hit their targets. All of the aircraft returned safely beginning at about 0516 (local time).

In the first day of the air war it was reported by the Navy that they were flying about one third of the overall attack sorties being flown by US air forces. The Six Navy carriers launched 226 sorties during the opening hours of the air campaign. Most of these were against command and control facilities, airfields and surface-to-air missile (SAM) sites, as well as troop emplacements. All of these attacks were executed in conjunction with Air Force and Marine Corps, as well as other allied air forces.

Surface-to-surface missile sites, primarily mobile Scud launchers, received the highest priority. The Joint Command was concerned with eliminating the surface-to-surface missile sites because of the international repercussions that missile attacks on other countries might cause. SAM sites were important in the plan to keep American casualties as low as possible.

A Tomcat RIO's view during in-flight refueling. USN

A-6E Intruders from the aircraft carriers *Ranger* and *Midway* attacked and sank three Iraqi *Osa*-class (Soviet built) patrol boats as the boats left the Iraqi naval base at Umm Qasr. The patrol boats were hit with Harpoon antiship missiles in much the same way as the Libyan and Iranian patrol craft had been knocked out in 1986 and 1988. The Iraqi patrol craft represented only a limited threat to US Navy forces operating in the Gulf. They are capable of carrying Styx missiles, which are reputed to have a twenty-five-mile range. These operations were conducted in support for an attempted amphibious landing on the coast of Kuwait. From the opening moments of the shooting war against Iraq the United States conducted operations in support of an amphibious operation that from the outset was presumed to be inevitable.

The nighttime operations were mainly carried out by the A-6E Intruders and the FA-18 Hornets. Day strikes were performed by the A-7 Corsair IIs and AV-8B Harriers. F-14 Tomcats provided fighter cover for both.

US Marine Corps AV-8B Harriers operating from the amphibious ship USS *Nassau* conducted primarily daylight strike operations, again in support of what was to be the largest amphibious landing since D-Day in World War II. The *Nassau*, flagship for Admiral LaPlante, was loaded down with twenty Harriers, all operational, as opposed to the six to eight aircraft normally carried. The Harriers, well-suited for support operations, were from the Marine Corps Air Wing stationed at Cherry Point and New River, both not far from Camp Lejune, North Carolina.

The Navy strike pilots were putting into practice the lessons learned at the strike warfare center, Fallon, Nevada. EA-6B Prowlers launched HARM (high-speed antiradiation missiles), which were directed at Iraqi radar and air defense sites. With the radar and SAM sites neutralized the attack aircraft (Intruders, Corsair IIs and Hornets) come in with laser-guided ordnance to achieve strikes with pin-point precision against command and control centers and communications infrastructures.

Conventional iron bombs of 500, 1,000 and 2,000 lb., as well as cluster bomb ordnance, were dropped on troop emplacements, vehicle storage areas, airfields and most importantly, mobile Scud missile sites.

An F-14 Tomcat refueling. USN

The first casualty of the air campaign happened when an FA-18 from the USS *Saratoga* was shot down over Iraq by a SAM. The pilot was identified as Lt. Comdr. Michael Speicher, thirty-three, of Jacksonville, Florida.

Early on 18 January, the Navy lost an A-6E Intruder. The crew members were identified as Lt. Robert Wetzel, thirty, and Lt. Jeffrey N. Zaun, twenty-eight.

American defense officials stressed that the campaign had just begun and more casualties were inevitable.

Said President Bush of the action on the first day of the war, "There will be problems, there will be setbacks, there will be more sacrifice." He went on to say, "We will stay the course, and we will succeed."

In Riyadh, General Schwarzkopf presided over the first of his now-famous press conferences in which he was narrator to some of the most amazing footage to come out of the war.

A senior American official of the air campaign against Iraq said, "We've been at war for a day, and some of the crews have already made

An F-14 Tomcat over rough terrain. USN

more than one run on Iraq . . . It's not a wave of bombings. It's round-the-clock . . . minute-by-minute."

AV–8B Harrier at sunset aboard the USS Nassau.
USN

An FA–18 of VFA–86 on the USS America. USN/Rice

Chapter 4

The Carrier Air War

While the scope of this chapter is the air war as it was conducted by the carrier air wings (CAW) of the US Navy and other naval air activities, we must not lose sight of the air war as it was practiced in its entirety. That is to say that it was above all things a joint operation.

Both tactically and logistically the naval air assets were operating under a joint plan of

The Saratoga *as seen from the* Kennedy *during Desert Storm.* USN

action whose ultimate goal was for the benefit of the total war aims, which were centrally controlled. In one of his news conferences, General Schwarzkopf said that the air war would be fought in four phases: air superiority, supression of air defenses, destruction of Iraqi army targets in Kuwait and air support of ground operations.

The desired effect of the Goldwater-Nichols military reform act of 1986 was to reduce and eliminate, if that was possible, the petty and destructive interservice rivalries and jealousies that had hobbled joint operations in the past. Desert Storm/Desert Shield was proof positive that the lessons of past mistakes had been learned by the commanders and war fighters of today's battles.

As the air war continued at a pace that was to average 2,000 sorties a day (this figure includes all types of missions, including reconnaissance support and supply), with the Navy accounting for about one third of them.

By the end of the first week the number had dropped down to 800 sorties a day because of bad weather and poor visibility over the target areas. The bad weather and poor visibility hindered the vital bomb damage assessment (BDA) by both aerial reconnaissance and satellite.

The same television technology that enabled the broadcast media to be on top of a story and transmit it for broadcast immediately gave the military commanders on all levels almost immediate feedback on what they had done in the skies over enemy-held territory. Smart technology gave a completely new face to the war and the air war in particular.

For the Navy the chief reconnaissance tool was the TARPS (tactical airborne reconnaissance pod system). The TARPS is a pod—that is, an external device that is an add-on to the underside of the forward fuselage—12 ft. long and weighing 1,700 lb. The TARPS pod contains two cameras and an infrared sensor. The system consists of one KS-87 frame camera, one KA-99 panoramic camera and one AAD/5 infrared system. On some photo-reconnaissance missions, especially those flown over Iraq, the KA-99 panoramic camera was removed and replaced with a KA-153 frame camera. The KA-153 is similar to the KA-99 but is a longer range camera that is intended to be used at higher altitudes. It provides extremely high resolution with a viewing field that stretches from ten to twenty miles.

The only criticism of these systems is that tactical intelligence is too slow. Photo-reconnaissance aircraft have to take the pictures, return to base, have the film developed and get it dis-

F-14 Tomcats stretch out over the flight deck of the USS Kennedy. USN

tributed. This all takes time, and in an air campaign time is a luxury that no one has.

Remotely Piloted Vehicles

Another of the television eye success stories was the Pioneer remotely piloted vehicle (RPV). Built by Israel Aircraft Industries (IAI), it was intended for use by the Marine Corps and the Navy. It was very much a response to real-world difficulties encountered during the ill-fated Marine deployment in Lebanon in 1982–1983. While the Marines had the fire support of the battleship *New Jersey*'s 16-in. guns, they lacked effective fire control and target spotting, both of which were crucial in the crowded hills of Lebanon. The use of ground troops or manned aerial spotters would prove costly in our most valuable resource, human lives.

It took several years, however, before the bugs were worked out and the system became

A TARPS pod is installed on an F–14 Tomcat on the USS Theodore Roosevelt. *These pods were used to take tactical-reconnaissance photos after air strikes.* USN

fully operational, but once that happened the United States had an extremely efficient and inexpensive reconnaissance and targeting system at its disposal.

About fifty Pioneer RPV were operated during Desert Storm: one each aboard the battleships *Wisconsin* and *Missouri*, one with the amphibious task force, two on land with the Marine Corps and one with the US Army. The RPVs carried on the *Wisconsin* and *Missouri* were in a manner of speaking hand-me-downs. They came from the battleships *Iowa* and *New Jersey*, which were decommissioned while the *Wisconsin* and *Missouri* were deployed in the Gulf. The RPVs were operated around the clock with great success. In daytime they were equipped with a video camera and at night they were equipped with a high-resolution infrared camera installed. The RPVs are in fact large radio-controlled model airplanes with a 17-ft. wingspan, powered by a small 26-hp gasoline engine capable of speeds up to 115 mph, and flying at 2,000 to 15,000 ft. They are virtually inaudible and invisible. The system is generally operated by a crew of twenty-two. Of the 40 or 50 RPVs operating in Desert Storm, about five were lost. Two were shot down over enemy territory, two returned with battle damage and one suffered engine failure and was deliberately crashed into the ground to keep it from falling into enemy hands intact.

The beauty of this system is in the thousands of hours of continued operations, with exceptionally fine qualitative results, while not one life was lost and no one was taken prisoner.

Through the use of technology the entire nature of modern warfare had changed. On 17 January, two FA-18 pilots from VFA-81 attacking an enemy target over Iraq were attacked by two Iraqi MiG-21s. The FA-18s turned, engaged the two MiGs, locked on, fired missiles and shot down the two Iraqi aircraft and resumed their bomb runs where they had left off, scoring direct

The Pioneer RPV (remotely piloted vehicle) was used in combat by US forces for the first time during Desert Storm. Arnold Meisner/Defense Image

hits with their ordnance loads and successfully completing their assigned missions.

In the old days they would have had to drop their bomb loads in order to engage the hostile fighters, thus aborting their bombing missions.

No military and naval force ever fielded had the benefit or the ability of satellite reconnaissance, communications, targeting and locating, as well as the ability to combine and integrate all of that with computerization and numerous electronic systems and sensors so as to completely control the battlefield.

An A-6 Intruder launches a SLAM (Standoff Land Attack Missile). The missile, a derivative of the successful Harpoon, was one of the standouts of Desert Storm. USN

The military aims of Operation Desert Storm, according to the Bush administration, were the liberation of Kuwait and the systematic dismantling of Saddam Hussein's military machine. It was estimated that the Iraqi air force had 750 to 800 aircraft and was flying 230 to 250 sorties a day before the beginning of hostilities. By the end of the first week the coalition air forces declared air superiority. Forty-one Iraqi aircraft had been destroyed (nineteen in aerial combat and twenty-two on the ground), and the Iraqi air force had been reduced to flying thirty to forty sorties a day, many of which were attempts to flee the battle zone.

Hunting Scud Launchers

As the weather cleared the sorties continued and everything went according to plan, with one big exception. Bombers had to be diverted from other missions to search out mobile Scud missile launchers in Iraq's eastern and western desert. Starting on the second day of the conflict Iraq had been launching Scud missiles at cities in Israel and Saudi Arabia. While the Scuds caused relatively minimal damage, their significance politically was much larger. In order to preserve the unity of the coalition forces it was necessary for the Bush administration to ensure that the Israelis restrain themselves militarily.

The job of searching for the missile sites fell mainly to the pilots on the carriers in the Red Sea. They spent a lot of time over western Iraq in search of Scud missiles and their launchers.

Another key aspect in the success of the air campaign was the ability to achieve more "jointness" in air operations. The importance of this aspect was evident to House Armed Services Committee head, Representative Les Aspin (D-Wisconsin), who said, "Basically, jointness doesn't mean everybody has to have an equal share of the action... You have Navy aircraft off carriers going to Air Force bases to refuel, allowing them to carry more munitions... That is something I dare to say we would not have done a few years ago."

Not only was this a triumph for jointness within the American military establishment, but we were operating closely with over a half a dozen different air forces, with great success. In addition to USAF and USMC aircraft, Navy aircraft operated in the skies with British, French, Saudi Arabian, Free Kuwaiti, Canadian and Italian air forces.

SLAM

The Navy scored another first on 18 January with its successful use of the heretofore experimental SLAM (standoff land attack missile). The SLAM, an improved version of the Navy's Harpoon, provided a new punch in the Navy's attack capability. SLAM had undergone its first test firing in July 1990 and was not supposed to go into service until August 1991.

Two SLAM missiles were fired at a heavily defended Iraqi military installation, and they both scored very dramatic direct hits—the kind of video that makes the evening news. The missiles were fired from A–6E Intruders from the *Saratoga* and were guided to their targets by A–7 Corsair II aircraft from the USS *John F. Kennedy*. The video showed the first missile striking the target squarely, and the second missile's video shows it going into the hole in the wall of the target made by the first missile—impressive by any standards, especially when one considers that the attacking aircraft were more than fifty miles away from their target when they launched the SLAMs.

The SLAM, manufactured by the McDonnell-Douglas Corporation, is constructed entirely of

Inside the aircraft carrier's hangar deck. USN

A lineup of FA-18s. USN

off-the-shelf technology and parts, which make it all the more desirable, especially from an acquisition viewpoint. The missile consists of a Harpoon missile's airframe, propulsion system and control system; the Maverick missile's infrared guidance system; and the Walleye laser-guided bomb's data link. A global positioning system satellite receiver was installed to update the missile's course while in flight.

While in flight, the satellite receiver gives an updated position report to the SLAMs navigation system. Once the missile is close to the target, a television camera in the nose lets the controller see where it is going. A video image is sent back to the aircraft's radar scope through the data link.

The data link is not activated until the missile is close to the target, to avoid jamming by enemy countermeasures. The video picture is sent back to the controlling aircraft where the pilot locks in on a specific aiming point. The

An F-14 Tomcat prepares to take off on a TARPS reconnaissance mission over Iraq. USN

aiming point can be as small as a window or a door.

At this point it is possible to launch a SLAM from an FA-18 or an A-6E, each of which can carry up to four SLAMs, and it can be guided into the target by either an A-6E, FA-18 or A-7.

The importance of using standoff weapons like the SLAM is in attacking heavily defended targets. When using the other laser-guided precision weapons like the Walleye or Paveway laser-guided bombs or the Maverick and Skipper laser-guided missiles, they must be launched from inside a twenty-mile radius from the target, which puts the attackers within the range of SAMs. In pressing home their attacks the attackers are bound to suffer higher casualties than if they had SLAMs.

POWs

If there is one soft spot in the American military attack plan it is in the desire and necessity to sustain as few casualties as possible. This

On the USS America, *a FOD (foreign object damage) walk-down during Operation Desert Storm.* USN/Rice

A-6 Intruder

The Intruder along with the Air Force's B-52 Stratofortress have one particular and peculiar thing in common besides the obvious fact that they are both employed in dropping bombs on things. During the Desert Storm campaign both the A-6s and the B-52s that saw combat were in many cases older than the pilots who flew them.

The Intruder was built to a 1957 requirement that was written to find a replacement for the venerable piston-engined Skyraider. The Intruder first flew on 19 April 1960. Designed by a Grumman design team headed by Lawrence Mead, it was the first attack aircraft for which the manufacturer of the airframe was also responsible for the manufacture of the onboard weapons systems.

It took three years for the first Intruders to enter active service with attack-squadron VA-42 in June of 1963. The Intruder first flew into combat in Vietnam off the USS *Independence* with the VA-75 "Sunday Punchers" on 1 July 1965. The Intruder scored many successes in the skies over North and South Vietnam, flying mainly in the all-weather attack role. During the Vietnam years there were 482 A-6As in service, and it was during this period that some of these aircraft were converted to other special purpose versions that were to begin the long progression of Intruder variations and derivatives. Three of these airframes

Even though many of the A-6 Intruders that fought over Kuwait and Iraq are older than the pilots who flew them, the Intruder is still the Navy's best attack bomber. This Intruder is loaded with 1,000-lb. bombs for its next mission off the Kennedy. USN

became the prototypes for what would eventually become the EA-6B Prowler electronic-warfare version, probably the most distinctive and successful of the Intruder derivatives, and one that would prove exceptionally effective in the Desert Storm campaign.

In 1971 the first KA-6Ds tankers made their appearance with VA-196 and were an immediate success in extending the operational range of Intruders and other Navy aircraft. With its spacious fuselage the Intruder was an ideal aircraft for the tanker role, taking over the job from some of the older carrier types such as the AD-3 Skywarrior. The KA-6Ds were made out of a number of A-6s with high-time airframes.

The success of the Intruder was not limited to only the US Navy pilots, but by the end of the war in and over Vietnam the Intruder was also flying with the US Marine Corps off carrier decks and also from land-based units. Combined Navy and Marine Corps losses of Intruders over Vietnam totaled sixty-nine aircraft of all versions.

The A-6E first flew in February of 1970 and flew operationally with VA-85 in 1972, too late to see action over Vietnam. The A-6E was and is the final production version of the Intruder. There have been 187 A-6Es built with a further 240 aircraft converted to A-6Es from other variants. With upgrades in the onboard computer system and avionics packages, and a new inventory of weapons systems, the Intruder has been able to maintain its role as the Navy's primary attack bomber. The Intruder scored firsts with its use of the air-launched Harpoon missile against Libyan and Iranian ships, and with the SLAM (Standoff Land Attack Missile), a Harpoon derivative, against Iraqi targets during Desert Storm.

Over the years the total of Intruders built is 695.

Now that the attack role will be handled by the FA-18 variants, and with the cancellation of the futuristic, stealthy A-12 Avenger project, and the AX attack aircraft way off in the future, it would appear that there is still some more time left for the Intruder.

includes having as few fliers as possible taken prisoner. The American public and families of those taken prisoner during the Vietnam War suffered greatly (as did those taken prisoner). When an American Navy pilot was taken prisoner in Lebanon in 1982 (his release was later secured by Jesse Jackson when Jackson personally intervened by going to Lebanon), we realized that the problem was still an active one and had not gone away.

On 21 January Iraqi television released the first video of seven captured coalition fliers; among them was Navy Lt. Jeffrey N. Zaun. Zaun was badly bruised and sullen. In subsequent videos released by the Iraqis, captured fliers, including Zaun, made statements that were critical of the coalition's effort and war aims. Rather than being incriminating for the fliers who made the statements, the world knew them for what they were. The international community was outraged: Saddam Hussein was ignoring international norms on the treatment of prisoners of war and ignoring the Geneva Convention.

The concern that the Navy placed on the issue of POWs is evidenced by the fact that they immediately assigned two officers to the parents of Lieutenant Zaun to act as spokespersons and intermediaries between the Zaun family and members of the press, many of whom were attempting to contact the Zaun family for statements.

Two FA-18s were listed as shot down on 17 January with both pilots listed as MIA.

Two A-6 Intruders were listed as lost on 18 January with one crewmember listed as POW and three as MIA.

One F-14 Tomcat was listed as shot down on 21 January with one crewmember rescued and one MIA.

Also lost during the air war was one CH-46 and one SH-60 helicopter, both of which were noncombat losses.

The lineup of FA–18s on the USS America. USN/Briggs

On 21 January Air Force Search and Rescue personnel rescued a Navy F-14 pilot downed in the desert in southern Iraq. On 24 January an Air Force F-16 pilot shot down into the sea on a mission over Kuwait was rescued by the LAMPS helicopter of the frigate USS *Nicholas*. The *Nicholas*, deployed off the Kuwaiti coast with HH-60H helicopters, embarked specifically for

Mk. 84 2,000-lb. bombs. These were the largest conventional ordnance carried on aircraft carriers. Note the message on the bombs. USN/Posnecker

search and rescue. The Navy disclosed that it was operating at least two helicopter special support squadrons for combat search and rescue missions during Desert Storm. The combat search and rescue teams were the only ones that were capable of operating inside of enemy-held Kuwait and Iraq.

The Navy was also operating one squadron of MH-53 helicopters in the mine counter-measures role. The helicopters operating with squadron HMM-14 were deployed with the USS *Tripoli* and engaged in the clearing of mines off the Kuwaiti coast in preparation for the anticipated amphibious assault.

Additional Navy helicopter detachments were assigned to various supply ships and provided extensive vertical replenishment operations. The helicopters, primarily CH-46 Sea Knights, delivered everything from spare parts and equipment to food and anything else that

An F-14 Tomcat of VF-102 Diamondbacks kicks in its afterburner during takeoff on the USS America *in action in the Red Sea during air operations for Desert Storm.* USN/Chichonowicz

was in short supply. Among the most important of deliveries was the absolutely voluminous quantities of mail for all the ships at sea. From Christmas packages to letters addressed "to any sailor," mail was the link with those back home.

On 22 January a Navy A-6E seriously damaged an Iraqi mine layer and another enemy ship in the Persian Gulf. Two other Iraqi ships fled. Also on the twenty-second another A-6E attacked and sank an Iraqi patrol boat near an oil platform in the Gulf.

On 23 January a Navy A-6E sank an Iraqi patrol boat and a Hovercraft and disabled a civilian Iraqi tanker that was conducting surveillance of allied aircraft that were attacking Iraq and Kuwait.

By the end of the first two weeks of the air campaign it was announced that the Navy had conducted 3,200 sorties, which represented

Replenishment at sea (RAS). The crew on the hangar deck replenishment station await recovery of an air-craft replacement engine as it is transferred to the USS America. USN/Briggs

about ten percent of the overall combat figures. This was down from the thirty percent totals that were stated earlier.

While the Navy pilots were busy striking targets inland in both Iraq and Kuwait, the Marine Corps AV-8B Harriers were operating in support of the anticipated amphibious landing. The AV-8B Harriers are not equipped with the sophisticated radar that the Navy and Air Force strike aircraft have and were limited to operating in daylight and clear weather conditions. During these operations two Harriers were lost. One was shot down over Kuwait on 28 January, and the other was lost making a landing onboard the USS *Nassau*. This was the *Nassau*'s only casualty of the whole campaign.

The Iraqi navy, never really a threat at sea, was virtually annihilated by strikes by A-6E

UNREP (underway replenishment): The carrier America loads up on fuel. USN/Briggs

Intruders and British Lynx helicopters operating from the destroyers *Cardif* and *Gloucester* with coordination from US frigates. The Lynx helicopters scored hits with Sea Skua and Penguin air-to-surface missiles. The US A–6E Intruder air strikes came from the carriers *Midway* and *Ranger* operating off the Iraqi coast in the Persian Gulf.

A few months earlier, the *Independence* had entered the Persian Gulf for the first time amid raised eyebrows and predictions of doom. Now the Persian Gulf was the area of operations for up to four carriers, not to mention the *Nassau*, which was operating in the role of a light carrier. The Gulf had become a very crowded place.

On 27 January A–6 Intruders sank two Iraqi naval vessels in the Bubiyan Channel and also struck at the Iraqi naval base at Umm Qasr. An Iraqi patrol boat in Kuwait City harbor was also hit and left burning. Six aircraft from the *Roose-*

Sunrise on the Persian Gulf. An FA–18 on the USS America. USN/West

An EA–6B Prowler from VAQ–137 during Desert Storm. USN

An airborne E–2C Hawkeye of the VAW–123 "Screwtops" from USS America. USN

velt hit troop positions inside Iraq with virtually no opposition.

On 28 January FA-18 Hornets operating from the USS *Theodore Roosevelt* in the Persian Gulf knocked out two Silkworm missile sites and an oil storage facility, as well as striking at Iraqi Republican Guards positions.

On 30 January British Lynx helicopters destroyed six Iraqi patrol craft in the northern Persian Gulf.

In February the pace of the war quickened with the Navy flying more strikes against Iraqi army units and emplacements rather than long-range missions against strategic targets.

The Navy reported the loss of an A-6E Intruder on 2 February. The aircraft was from VA-36 on the *Theodore Roosevelt*. The crew members were identified as Lt. Patrick Connor, twenty-five, and Lt. Comdr. Barry Cooke, thirty-five. Both men were killed in the crash.

On 6 February an F-14 from VF-1, aboard the *Saratoga*, destroyed an Iraqi Mi-8 helicopter.

On 15 February an A-6E Intruder aircraft crashed during a landing attempt on the aircraft carrier *America*. The crew ejected safely, but the aircraft was a total loss and was pushed over the side.

The Navy was still operating around the clock from six aircraft carriers. Supplies and spare parts were not a problem. The aircraft carriers were equipped with ninety days' worth of spares, and the embarked air groups were also reinforced, carrying extra pilots and aircraft. While most of the fighter and attack

F-14s and FA-18s on the Theodore Roosevelt. USN

squadrons were listed as having twelve aircraft assigned, in reality most squadrons carried a few extra pilots and had, generally speaking, a couple of spare aircraft. (See the appendix on air wings and note that the figures on the air wings in the appendix do not include any of the spares.)

Back in the United States the Navy was making preparations to reinforce the six carriers deployed should it become necessary. The USS *Forrestal* went out on a Caribbean workup—should more help be needed she would be the next to go. The Navy also announced that the *Nimitz* and *Eisenhower* were being made ready.

The long-awaited ground war began on 24 February. With dazzling success on the ground, the air war became subordinated and put into step by the overall objectives of the campaign. (That is not to say that the air war was not part of the program.) Until the first moment that ground troops stepped off, the most important issues were whether there would actually be a ground war, and the converse of that question, could the job (total war) be done with airpower alone.

An FA-18 of VFA-87 prepares for launch to provide close air support from the aircraft carrier Theodore Roosevelt. *USN*

The questions themselves are the legacies of World War II and Vietnam. With the emergence of airpower as the dominant technology both strategically and tactically, what was the role of forces on land? Do wars really need to be won on the ground? The answer once again was yes!

The missions continued as they had—twenty-four hours a day, every day. The statistics for the Navy in the air war were impressive—over 16,000 sorties—which meant about 50,000 flight hours logged and thousands of tons of bombs dropped.

One of the most important facts, which is also a real illustrator of the effectiveness of the air war from the Navy's perspective, is the fact that in a war that lasted for forty-two days the Navy did not lose a single aircraft after the eighteenth day. On the last day of the fighting the Navy flew 660 sorties from its six carriers, four of which were now operating in the Persian Gulf.

The air war in its last stages got even more frantic than it had been. "It's like shooting ducks in a barrel" was the description of the situation over the target area, with the Iraqi army in full retreat along the highway that led back to Iraq from Kuwait—the now famous "Highway of Death." The Navy pilots were flying multiple missions, receiving the targeting information on their way back out to their aircraft.

During the air war the USS *America* was ordered to steam from its position in the Red Sea

An F-14 Tomcat leaves the deck of the aircraft carrier Theodore Roosevelt. USN

and take up a position in the Persian Gulf along with the aircraft carriers *Midway, Ranger* and *Theodore Roosevelt*, creating what became known as Battle Force Zulu. The *Saratoga* and *John F. Kennedy* remained on station in the Red Sea. *America* became the only carrier to operate in both the Red Sea and the Persian Gulf. The *America* air wing went into combat within one day of arriving on station in both the Red Sea and Persian Gulf areas, including strike missions against almost 150 targets in both Iraq and Kuwait. Their combat sorties included arduous long-range missions across Iraqi territory while operating from the Red Sea. Missions from the Persian Gulf were characterized by shorter distances, which allowed for a greater number of combat sorties to be flown per day.

The Navy was using all of the assets at its disposal. Because there was no submarine threat to speak of, the Navy was deploying the S-3 Viking aircraft in roles that it had never been intended to fulfill. The S-3 Viking proved its versatility performing in-flight refueling, electronic support and bombing missions, carrying Rockeye cluster bombs. There is also some mention of the S-3 carrying the air-launch version of the Harpoon, and it presents itself as a possible launch platform for the SLAM—if not now, then eventually.

The P-3C Orion was also active in Desert Shield operations. Normally an antisubmarine aircraft, the Orion was used in the surface-search role for which it is well suited. The Orion, which is based on the civilian DC-6 airframe and powerplant, is capable of spending long hours in the air (over water) at low levels. The P-3Cs were also used to search for mines.

Cease-Fire

On 27 February President Bush announced a cease-fire, and the air war ceased, although the Navy continued flying defensive missions.

On the same day the RPV from the battleship *Wisconsin* detected two Iraqi military boats

An S–3B Viking landing on the Theodore Roosevelt. *The multi-mission Viking was one of the success stories of Desert Storm.* USN

fleeing Faylaka Island. The boats were reportedly carrying members of the Iraqi Secret Police. The fleeing boats were destroyed by Navy attack aircraft.

On 1 March an RPV overflight on Faylaka Island detected hundreds of Iraqi soldiers running after it on the ground; they were waving a white flag and attempting to surrender. This was the first time troops of one nation ever attempted to surrender to a crewless, unarmed aircraft.

During Operation Desert Storm the Navy lost five A-6s, one F-14 and three FA-18s in combat. Such light losses in the face of the heavy antiaircraft fire over Iraq and Kuwait is tribute to the excellence of US Navy pilots and crews.

The final statistics for the number of sorties flown and the tonnage of ordnance dropped were very impressive indeed. USS *America*'s Carrier Air Wing One flew more than 3,000 sorties and dropped 2,000 tons. USS *John F. Kennedy*'s Carrier Air Wing Three flew more than 2,900 sorties and dropped 1,750 tons. USS *Miday*'s Carrier Air Wing Five flew more than 4,000 sorties and dropped 1,500 tons. USS *Ranger*'s Carrier Air Wing Two flew more than 4,200 sorties and dropped 2,100 tons. USS *Saratoga*'s Carrier Air Wing Seventeen flew more than 2,600 sorties and dropped 2,150 tons. USS *Theodore Roosevelt*'s Carrier Air Wing Eight flew more than 4,200 sorties and dropped 2,750 tons.

A US Marine Corps AV–8B Harrier conducting air operations during Desert Storm. The aircraft are from the USS Nassau. *DoD*

The gun crew of turret number one of the battleship
Wisconsin. Arnold Meisner/Defense Image

Chapter 5

The Surface War

The commander of Destroyer Squadron 24 (DESRON 24) was Capt. Jim Hinkle, who with his staff participated in the multinational maritime interception operation in support of United Nations resolutions 661 and 665. Captain Hinkle was the on-scene commander for the Red Sea interception operation. The Red Sea force participated in more than 900 merchant vessel boardings and virtually closed down the port of Aqaba, Jordan, as a transshipment port to Iraq.

DESRON 24 also planned and coordinated the highly successful boarding of two uncooper-

Aerial view of the USS San Jacinto *Aegis guided-missile cruiser.* USN

ative merchant vessels by helicopter insertion of specially trained Navy SEAL teams. Ships from France, Greece and Spain combined with Hinkle's forces to control all shipping in the northern Red Sea.

With the outbreak of hostilities, DESRON 24 was assigned the coordination of air defense for the Mediterranean theater of operations. The multinational forces were brought together to provide air defense for the millions of tons of equipment and supplies being shipped to Desert Storm forces by the Military Sealift Command. DESRON 24 also ensured the safe transit of the thousands of airlift flights that crossed the Mediterranean skies en route to Saudi Arabia.

The DESRON 24 staff was normally accustomed to tactical antisubmarine operations, but found themselves engaged in a variety of efforts that had nothing to do with ASW.

The frigate *Elmer Montgomery* departed Mayport on 7 August and cleared the Straight of Gibraltar on the sixteenth. En route to the Suez Canal the *Montgomery* briefly participated in two NATO exercises, Display Determination 90 and National Week 90. The exercises were designed to test and improve NATO's multinational operations at sea.

On 23 August the *Montgomery* made its initial southbound transit through the Suez Canal into the northern Red Sea and immediately commenced maritime interdiction force operations. At the time the operations were designed to support Operation Desert Shield and implement the United Nations resolutions. From the time that it left Mayport until the time that it completed its first tour of duty it was under way for seventy-eight days. *Montgomery* fired the first shots by a US ship making a maritime interception. *Montgomery* also had the distinction of making the 2,500th interception by US Naval forces, as well as completing fifty boardings of merchant vessels.

On 27 October the *Montgomery* returned to the Mediterranean for required maintenance

The decks of the battleship USS Wisconsin. Arnold Meisner

and also to participate in more NATO exercises. During this time *Montgomery* participated in search and rescue operations with French naval forces to rescue the crew of a sinking sailing vessel.

On Thanksgiving Day 1990 the *Montgomery* transited the Suez Canal southbound to resume interdiction operations with the *Saratoga* battle group in the northern Red Sea.

On 9 January 1991 *Montgomery* participated in her 100th boarding operation.

On 10 January *Montgomery* returned to the Mediterranean to join in operations to ensure the security of the Suez Canal. While in port at Catania, Italy, Comdr. Fred G. Orchard relieved Comdr. Robert A. Higgins as commanding officer. During its assignment to the Suez Canal protection operations *Montgomery* was assigned as sector anti-air warfare commander for nineteen days, an unusual assignment for a frigate.

Onboard the *Montgomery* throughout her deployment were the helicopters of HSL–36 Detachment 9.

While Desert Storm operations were of primary importance, the operations in the Mediterranean are not to be dismissed lightly. They had an important place in the overall tapestry of events. With countries like Libya, Algeria and Tunisia, as well as Lebanon, all bordering on the Mediterranean and terrorist activity anticipated, protecting American interests and lines of supply were a vital if not unheralded aspect of Desert Storm operations.

There were very real fears that there might be some form of intervention by the Libyan or Sudanese governments, both of whom had been friendly if not outright supportive to Saddam Hussein and hostile to the coalition's aims. Coalition forces needed to display a flexibility that would allow an appropriate armed response should one be required. The British government eventually deployed the aircraft carrier HMS *Ark Royal* to the Eastern Mediterranean to provide an additional armed presence in the general area. The *Ark Royal* operated jointly with a US Navy escort.

The Mediterranean became an area where noncombat logistics, support and repair ships were stationed.

Accompanying the *Saratoga* and making her first deployment, the USS *Philippine Sea* made the Atlantic transit at flank speed, transiting the Suez Canal and taking up station in the northern Red Sea where *Philippine Sea* participated also in maritime interdiction operations. During one such boarding inspection *Philippine Sea* found a cargo of chemicals that could be used in the manufacture of chemical weapons. The cargo was headed for a company located in Jordan. After further investigation it was learned that the company in question also had offices in Baghdad. The ship and its cargo were diverted and not allowed to offload in Jordan.

In other instances when two merchant ships refused to stop for inspection of their cargoes *Philippine Sea* fired both 5-in. and .50-cal. shells until both ships were boarded by SEAL teams fastroped from helicopters.

After the first month and a half on station *Philippine Sea* made the transit north, beginning a five-month cycle in which the ship would rotate between the northern Red Sea and the eastern Mediterranean every six weeks. The Mediterranean offered liberty ports as well as a two-week maintenance period during the Christmas holiday.

In January *Philippine Sea* rejoined the carrier groups in the northern Red Sea in time to take part in the shooting war. The ship programmed and fired Tomahawk cruise missiles during the initial phases of the offensive against Kuwait.

During deployment, life at sea assumes a constant routine: general quarters, eating, sleeping and standing watch.

In early February the *Philippine Sea* made her sixth and final transit of the Suez Canal, and in doing so became the first US Navy ship to make six Suez Canal transits in one deployment. The total length of her deployment was 234 days.

The USS *Sampson*, last of the *C.F. Adams*-class destroyers on its last deployment before its scheduled decommissioning later in 1991, left Mayport with the *Saratoga* on 7 August, making the transatlantic crossing in eight days. On 15 August it joined up with the Sixth Fleet in the Mediterranean before continuing eastward for an immediate southbound transit of the Suez Canal. Arriving on station in the Red Sea on 24 August, it immediately began maritime interdiction operations in support of the UN resolutions. On 26 August *Sampson* conducted the first boarding and search of a merchant vessel during Operation Desert Shield. Two days later *Sampson* participated in the first diversion of a merchant vessel to another port because the merchant ship was carrying prohibited cargo to Iraq.

On 21 September *Sampson* transited the Suez Canal northbound to take part in the NATO on-call forces exercise, and Display Determination 2–90 in the Mediterranean.

On 1 November the *Sampson* transited the Suez Canal southbound in order to join back up with the forces on patrol in the northern Red Sea. During its time at sea *Sampson* conducted more than sixty underway replenishments.

Sampson set sail on its first Mediterranean deployment back in 1965. In 1983 *Sampson* served as part of the Middle East Force, also off the coast of Lebanon. In October 1987 she served as part of the Navy's escort force in the Persian Gulf, escorting reflagged Kuwaiti tankers and other US flag merchant vessels.

The frigate USS *Thomas C. Hart*, commanded by Comdr. David C. Rollins, spent a total of 172 days at sea during its eight-month deployment. After its departure from Mayport on 7 August it headed directly for the Red Sea to begin operations with the maritime interdiction force. During its participation in Desert Storm and Desert Shield, *Hart* conducted forty-three boardings and over 300 interrogations of merchant vessels near the Gulf of Aqaba.

When hostilities broke out on 17 January *Hart* was on station with other members of the maritime interdiction force, where it participated in escorting logistics ships and multinational forces to the southern Red Sea, after which it returned north to continue its activities with the interdiction forces.

Hart made two transits to the Mediterranean where it participated in exercises with the NATO on-call force. While in the Red Sea during Desert Storm the *Hart* also operated as an escort ship for the aircraft carriers *Kennedy* and *America*, as well as the *Saratoga*, whose battle group *Hart* is normally assigned to.

When the cruiser USS *Biddle* sailed for the Middle East with the *Saratoga* battle group it steamed directly for the Suez Canal, which it transited on 24 August, for the first of its six transits of the Suez Canal. *Biddle* immediately assumed its position on station with the maritime interdiction force supporting the United Nations resolutions 661 and 665. *Biddle's* other assigned duties were to provide antiaircraft defense for the USS *Saratoga* and in the northern Red Sea.

On 10 September 1990 Capt. Louis F. Harlow relieved Capt. Grant D. Fulkerson while the *Biddle* was on station. Up to that point the *Biddle* had participated in three boardings, reportedly the first of which was the first boarding of an Iraqi ship during the Desert Shield phase of the operation.

On 12 September *Biddle* participated in its seventh boarding of a vessel, and this one resulted in its first diversion of a merchant vessel.

On the seventeenth the *Biddle* was the first American warship to participate in the boarding of a Soviet-flagged vessel. *Biddle* participated in boarding two more vessels before transiting the Suez Canal northbound on 20 September for a four-day port call at Izmir, Turkey. At this point *Biddle* had spent forty-nine consecutive days under way. After departing Izmir *Biddle* took part in the exercise Display Determination 90 for sixteen days where it was given the responsibility of Eagle Control air coordinator for the exercise.

On 15 October the *Biddle* arrived at Alexandria, Egypt, for a one-week intermediate maintenance availability (IMAV) with the destroyer tender USS *Yellowstone*.

From 22 to 23 October the *Biddle* transited the Suez Canal southbound to resume her station on the Red Sea.

Prior to the holidays the *Biddle* embarked a Coast Guard Law Enforcement Detachment (LEDET) and a CNN news team. By 4 December

Biddle had made a total of twenty-seven boardings and four diversions.

On 29 October the *Biddle* aided the merchant vessel *Sea Breeze*, which was on fire and sinking. An injured sailor was flown by the ship's helicopter to the USS *Mossbruger*, which had the nearest medical facilities. *Biddle*'s helicopter was from HSL–34 Detachment 1.

Biddle spent its Christmas in the port of Toulon, France, departing on 5 January 1991 and transiting the Suez Canal southbound on the ninth to arrive on station on the tenth. *Biddle* accumulated a total of thirty boardings by the time Desert Storm commenced on 17 January.

During Desert Storm *Biddle* made a total of six more boardings, including the only actual seizure of a ship.

Biddle departed the Red Sea on 11 March 1991 to return to the United States. When it departed it left with the highest percentage rate of diversions to boardings of any ship in the Multinational Interdiction Force (MIF), an impressive 22.2 percent.

Biddle's primary role in the Red Sea during Desert Storm was to provide antiaircraft defenses for the combined battle force of the USS *Saratoga* and USS *John F. Kennedy*, as well as

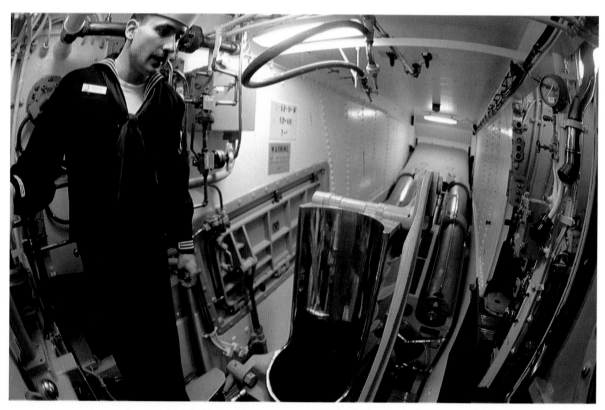

Inside turret number one on the battleship Wisconsin.
Arnold Meisner/Defense Image

the entire northern Red Sea. During this time *Biddle* coordinated over 850 aircraft interceptions with combat air patrol aircraft from the carriers *Saratoga*, *Kennedy* and *America*. *Biddle* also served as a test platform for the establishment of equipment parameters relating to the detection of aircraft in the intense conditions of heat and sand in the Red Sea. This was accomplished by using aircraft to fly at the USS *Biddle* to see where and when they could be detected and tracked on the radars.

During the course of the MIF operations *Biddle's* embarked helicopter detachment from HSL–34 Detachment 1 flew 375 sorties on all sorts of missions. Intended primarily for use in an ASW capacity and surface search role the *Biddle's* detachment of LAMPS II helicopters proved valuable in searching out merchant ships during the MIF operation.

On 13 March *Biddle* made its sixth and final transit of the Suez Canal after spending 136 days on station in the Red Sea. During this period the ship scored 100 percent on the completion of the requirements for the cruiser battle efficiency E competition. The *Biddle* spent 202 days under way in wartime conditions, including forty-nine days of combat operations. The forty-nine days in combat conditions is more than any other US Navy cruiser deployed in the Middle East crisis. The ship conducted fifty-one underway replenishments and eighteen vertical replenishments.

Wisconsin

No other single ship epitomizes the war at sea from a surface viewpoint as the battleship *Wisconsin*.

During the eight months that the battleship *Wisconsin* was deployed in the Persian Gulf it took part in every phase of Desert Storm/Desert Shield. Reinforced by the arrival in the Persian Gulf of the battleship USS *Missouri* in early January the *Wisconsin* departed Bahrain to take up its position prior to the start of hostilities. With *Wisconsin* acting as the Tomahawk Missile Strike Coordinator it fired a total of twenty-four Tomahawks over the course of two days and coordinated the launch of more than 200 Tomahawks assigned Persian Gulf strike missions.

Subsequently the *Wisconsin* also assumed responsibilities as the local antisurface warfare coordinator for the northern Persian Gulf surface action group.

During the air war the *Wisconsin* also served as a vital hub for logistics and personnel transportation in the central Persian Gulf. The *Wisconsin* operated as the central receiving point for passengers, mail and cargo headed for ships throughout the Persian Gulf, taking some of the pressure off the existing supply infrastructure. *Wisconsin* transferred over 40,000 lb. of mail, 20,000 lb. of cargo and 140 personnel. Throughout its deployment *Wisconsin* also served the fleet as an armored oiler helping to refuel and replenish the other ships in its group.

On 6 February *Wisconsin* relieved the battleship *Missouri* on the firing line off the coast of Kuwait. On its first fire mission *Wisconsin* fired eleven 16-in. shells into an Iraqi artillery battery located in southern Kuwait. The mission was called in by a Marine Corps OV–10 aircraft. On the following day *Wisconsin* fired twenty-four 16-in. rounds at an Iraqi communications facility, heavily damaging the site. The artillery spotting for this and subsequent fire support missions was provided by the ship's own RPV (remotely piloted vehicle).

On the evening of 7 February the *Wisconsin* was tasked with destroying Iraqi special forces boats at the Khavr al Mufattah Marina on the Kuwaiti coast. Using its RPV effectively, *Wisconsin* placed fifty 16-in. high-explosive projectiles into the target area, destroying several piers and fifteen small boats. Another nineteen 16-in. rounds exploded on suspected artillery batteries and command posts that same night in what were described as pre-arranged fire support missions.

On 8 February *Wisconsin* completed its first fire-support mission off the coast of Khafji, Saudi Arabia, where it fired against Iraqi artillery batteries, infantry bunkers and an Iraqi mechanized unit in support of US Marine ground operations. Twenty-nine rounds were fired on eight separate fire support missions. The ship's

Aegis Guided-Missile Cruiser
USS *San Jacinto*

Designed to be built on the *Spruance*-class destroyer hull, the Aegis guided-missile cruiser is one of the most sophisticated warships ever built. Originally intended as purely state-of-the-art antiaircraft protection for the carrier battle group, the Aegis-class cruiser has emerged as a platform for operations that are highly diversified. In Desert Storm, the *San Jacinto* was outfitted with a full load of Tomahawk cruise missiles, making her the Navy's first strike cruiser, a devastating and powerful weapons system.

The *San Jacinto*, built by the Ingalls Shipbuilding Corporation of Pascagula, Mississippi, is the lead ship of the third modification of the original Aegis design, and consequently is considered to be a much more powerful ship than the *Ticonderoga*, which was commissioned in 1984. The *San Jacinto* was commissioned in Houston, Texas, in January of 1986.

The Aegis combat system is what makes the *San Jacinto* one of the Navy's most capable surface combatants. At the heart of this system is the AN/SPY–1A radar, which is able to "see" in all directions simultaneously. Conventional mechanically rotating radars see a target only when the radar beam strikes it once in every 360–degree rotation of its antenna. A separate tracking radar then engages each target. In contrast, the computer-controlled AN/SPY–1A radar brings these and other functions together within one system. It can detect, track and engage hundreds of aircraft and missiles while continually watching the sky for new targets. The SPY radar is totally electronic with four fixed arrays sending out beams of electromagnetic energy in all directions simultaneously. Thus target detection to system response takes only a few seconds.

An Aegis display system, command and decision system and weapons control system

continued on page 98

The Aegis guided-missile cruiser USS San Jacinto *transits the Suez Canal southbound to enter the Red Sea.* San Jacinto *was carrying a full load of Tomahawk cruise missiles.* USN

combine to form the nucleus of the ship's combat information center, providing overall battle management and coordination for the entire carrier battle group. The command and decision system is the primary element through which the captain develops his battle doctrine. The weapons control system directs such weapons as the standard SN-2 surface-to-air missile, Tomahawk or Harpoon surface-to-surface cruise missiles, two 5-in. rapid-fire guns, air- and ship-launched antisubmarine torpedoes, two Phalanx Close-in Weapons Systems (CIWS) and two Sikorsky SH-60B Light Airborne Multi Purpose System (LAMPS) III helicopters.

The Aegis system can fire more rapidly and control in-flight more missiles than any other Navy shipboard system. The weapons systems are supplemented by sonar (active and passive), electronic-countermeasures decoys and passive detection systems, to help detect, classify and confuse enemy units and incoming weapons.

An operational readiness test system (ORTS) makes Aegis the only shipboard weapons system capable of constantly monitoring thousands of critical operating points. This system detects faults and provides maintenance data for rapid correction or repair by the ship's crew.

The Mk.41 Vertical Launch System (VLS) is a revolutionary new launching system capable of firing a mix of surface and airborne targets. It is modular in design with a series of cells symmetrically grouped to form a launcher magazine. Each module contains all necessary equipment for launching functions when interfaced with the Aegis combat system.

The primary air defense weapon is the SM-2 standard missile. The SM-2 is propelled by a dual-thrust rocket motor and incorporates a high-explosive warhead The 3,000-lb. SM-2 is always under the positive control of the Aegis combat system. SM-2's unique midcourse guidance and resistance to electronic jamming permits long range and high firepower.

The Mk.86 Gunfire Control System (GFCS) is the central subelement of the gun weapon system (GWS). It provides singular or dual remote control of the ship's forward and aft 5-in. gun mounts to engage up to two targets simultaneously. The GFCS conducts direct firing against surface radar and actually tracks targets, as well as indirect firing during naval gunfire support (NGFS). The Mk.45 5-in. gun mounts are located along the ship's centerline, one forward and one aft. Each of the shielded, unmanned and fully automatic mounts is capable of firing sixteen to twenty rounds per minute. Each mount can be controlled remotely by the GFCS or locally from the gun mount itself.

The AN/SQS-53B is the hull mounted sonar with the capability of both passive and active sonar operations. Its function is to provide long-range search capability, target detection, localization, classification and tracking of underwater contacts. In the active mode the AN/SQS-53B is able to provide target range, bearing and depth information for the external fire control system. In the passive mode the sonar is capable of searching in both the broadband, narrowband and acoustic noise ranges, then process and conduct spectral analysis and classification of the target.

The SQS-19 Tactical Towed Array Sonar (TACTAS) is a sonar that provides a long-range passive detection and tracking capability in a multitude of underwater tracking conditions. It gives 360-degree coverage and offers higher maximum search, launch, retrieval and survival speeds than previous towed array sonars. The TACTAS is integrated into the Aegis weapons system.

The ship's LAMPS III (SH-60B) helicopter greatly enhances the ship's antisubmarine capability, as well as providing the ship with increased surveillance, targeting and search and rescue capabilities.

The Phalanx CIWS provides the final defense against antiship missiles. In its primary role CIWS will automatically fire at antiship missiles that penetrate the ship's primary defense systems. There are two CIWS mounts located midships, one port and one starboard. Each CIWS mount contains all necessary electronics, search and tracking antennas and a six-barrel 20-mm. gatling gun capable of firing at a rate of 3,000 rounds per minute from its 980-round magazine.

RPVs were used to reconnoiter the Kuwaiti coast and interior, as well as Kuwait City and Faylaka Island. The information gathered here was extremely valuable in the planning of the ground offensive that was to happen later in February. *Wisconsin* operated throughout this period in coastal waters that were mine infested and within the range of Iraqi Silkworm missiles.

Between 9 and 20 February the *Wisconsin* returned to the central Persian Gulf so it could rearm, refuel and replenish. During this period it resumed its role as logistics hub for the Persian Gulf.

On 21 February *Wisconsin* returned to its place on the firing line off the coast of Saudi Arabia at Khafji, where it fired fifty 16-in. rounds into an Iraqi command complex. More than ten buildings were destroyed or heavily damaged in the barrage. The ship's RPV had spotted trucks resupplying the complex.

On 23 February the *Wisconsin* fired ninety-four 16-in. rounds at Iraqi infantry positions and artillery and command posts, as well as SAM sites. All this was in preparation for the ground offensive that was to start the next morning.

On 24 and 25 February *Wisconsin* fired twenty-three 16-in. rounds into two Iraqi bunker complexes. These two calls for fire supported the push up the Kuwaiti coast by coalition forces and paved the way for the continued push to Kuwait City.

As the ground campaign progressed the *Wisconsin* repositioned itself up the coast off of Kuwait City, having completed a twenty-hour transit through mine-infested waters. The ship

Battleship Wisconsin *turret number one showing Iraqi flag and shell marks for fire missions.* Arnold Meisner/Defense Image

99

arrived in position off the coast on the morning of 26 February.

From this position *Wisconsin* operated continuous RPV reconnaissance missions in support of the advancing coalition forces, and fired the last eleven rounds of 16-in. gunfire of the war.

Wisconsin remained on station for the next seven days while the coalition forces liberated and secured Kuwait City. The *Wisconsin* was released from its station in the northern Persian Gulf to make preparations to return home.

During *Wisconsin's* deployment it racked up some very impressive statistics. It fired a total of 528 16-in. rounds, 881 5-in. rounds, 5,200 20-mm. CIWS rounds and flew 348 RPV hours, 661 safe helicopter landings and steamed for a total of 46,000 miles. All of this without a single serious injury.

The battleship *Missouri* was used in forty-seven fire-support missions, firing a total of 759 16-in. rounds.

The newest of the warships deployed in Desert Storm/Desert Shield was the Aegis guided missile cruiser USS *Normandy*. It distinguished itself during Desert Storm by serving as the command platform for antiaircraft defense for the *America* battle group, providing comprehensive air surveillance and air traffic control in the airspace around the battle group. Additionally it successfully launched numerous Tomahawk cruise missiles against Iraqi targets and participated in Red Sea maritime interdiction operations.

The *Kalamazoo* refueled the *America* battle group during both Atlantic transits, as well as extensive battle group logistic support in both the Red Sea and the Persian Gulf.

On 18 January the frigate USS *Nicholas* (FFG-47) made the headlines when it attacked nine Kuwaiti oil platforms that were occupied by Iraqi soldiers. In the action *Nicholas* killed five Iraqi soldiers and captured twenty-three. The attack was begun by the ship's helicopter and the frigate's 76-mm. gun. The ship was then joined by a Saudi Arabian patrol boat and the two ships bombarded the seven other oil platforms.

The Iraqis had initially been firing on allied aircraft flying missions in the area. The twenty-three prisoners, including five wounded, were ferried to the ship by helicopter where they were interrogated, fed and washed. The prisoners seemed grateful to their captors, to be safe, and to be out of the war. From *Nicholas* the prisoners were ferried to the destroyer *Mossbruger*, and from there they were handed over to Marines on shore who ran temporary POW facilities, until they were eventually handed over to the Saudi military permanent POW facilities.

On 24 January Saudi Arabian naval forces fired a Harpoon at and sank an Iraqi mine-laying vessel in the northern Persian Gulf.

Amphibious Forces

Throughout all the action in the Gulf the amphibious force was standing at readiness, poised for the invasion that everyone knew had to come. Onboard the amphibs, the so-called gator freighters, the Marines practiced and got ready to go.

On 13 January the east coast amphibious units were joined by west coast amphibious units under the command of Rear Adm. Steven S. Clarey, Commander Amphibious Group Three, and elements of the Fifth Marine Expeditionary Brigade under the command of Brig. Gen. Peter J. Rowe. Task Force 156, commanded by Rear Admiral LaPlante, was now composed of forty-three ships: thirty-one amphibious ships, seven logistics ships and five maritime prepositioning force ships.

On 29 January 1991, an amphibious raid was flawlessly conducted by a subordinate element of the task force composed of Amphibious Squadron Five, with the USS *Okinawa*, USS *Ogden*, USS *Durham*, USS *Ft. McHenry* and USS *Cayuga* at the Iraqi-held Maradin Island off the coast of Kuwait.

As the ground war came to a halt and cease-fire talks commenced, amphibious operations continued in the north Arabian Gulf. Units of the Amphibious Group Alpha (Amphibious Squadron Five) and the 13th Marine Expeditionary Unit (MEU) evacuated over 1,400 Iraqi enemy prisoners of war from Faylaka Island. The small island located off the coast of Kuwait had been occupied since the beginning of the invasion.

As the redeployment stateside began for the east coast amphibious ships, Amphibious Group Three remained in theater until they were ordered to render assistance in a humanitarian relief mission to victims of the recent typhoon in Bangladesh.

Also remaining deployed on station were the cruiser *Virginia*, the destroyer *Perble*, the ammunition stores ship *Santa Barbara* and the destroyer *Pratt*, as well as the frigate *Halyburton*, all originally part of the *America* battle group.

The *America* battle group departed the Red Sea and transited the Suez Canal on the third of April 1991 on its way back home.

Environmental Terrorism

On 25 January Iraqis sabotaged the main Kuwaiti supertanker loading facility, sending millions of gallons of crude oil into the Gulf, killing wildlife and threatening the Saudi Arabian water desalinization facilities along the eastern coast of Saudi Arabia. It is estimated that the sabotaged oil facility was pumping 86 million barrels of oil a day into the Persian Gulf. So begins the world's first case of environmental terrorism, but this was only the beginning.

On 26 January the Navy announced that the *Los Angeles*-class submarine USS *Louisville* was the first submarine to launch a Tomahawk cruise missile in combat. In turn the USS *Pittsburgh* became the first Atlantic fleet submarine to go into action since World War II. While the Pentagon still has not released or commented on any further submarine operations, we know that both boats launched at least one Tomahawk cruise missile each.

Also on 26 January an Air Force F-111 planted a laser-guided bomb on the Kuwaiti oil pumping pier to stop the flow of oil into the Gulf.

The USS Gunston Hall *part of the amphibious force at sea.* USN

It was a success, but a very ominous glimpse of things to come. The oil spill, thought to be much greater than first estimated, is said to be 460 million gallons—that is to say, forty-two times greater than the largest US oil spill, the *Exxon Valdez* oil spill.

The largest Iraqi naval action happened on 29 January when an Iraqi minesweeper, two captured Kuwaiti missile boats and three Iraqi Polnochny (Soviet built) landing ships, each capable of carrying about 180 troops, were sunk in the northern Persian Gulf. It was believed that their destination was the reinforcement of Iraqi forces fighting in the vicinity of Khafji.

On 30 January, Gen. Norman Schwarzkopf announced that the Iraqi Navy lost forty-six of its fifty patrol craft. Iraq's naval forces have never been considered a threat to the US Navy. The most formidable ships are four *Lupo*-class corvettes that have never been delivered. They were built and purchased in Italy in the 1980s but at that time Iran made a public threat that it would sink them before they ever reached Iraq, so they and an oiler, also built in Italy, have remained in La Spezia ever since.

Also on the thirtieth the destroyer tender USS *Puget Sound* departed for the Gulf. Its intended purpose was the repair of any damaged US Navy ships should that situation arise.

On 12 February the battleship *Missouri* joined in with Marine Corps artillery in pounding Iraqi troop positions in southern Kuwait.

Mines

On 18 February both the amphibious helicopter carrier USS *Tripoli* and the Aegis guided-missile cruiser USS *Princeton* struck mines while operating off the coast of Kuwait. The ships were conducting mine-clearing operations when each struck submerged mines within three hours of each other. Both ships suffered extensive damage. At first it was believed that the *Tripoli* suffered the worst damage.

A CH–46 Sea Knight helicopter during vertical replenishment operations in the Gulf during Desert Storm. USN

103

Sailors onboard the *Tripoli* were thrown out of their berths by the early morning explosion. The ship sustained a 10x16 ft. hole about 10 ft. below the waterline. The crew had been told to expect large explosions ashore since the Air Force was dropping 15,000-lb. "daisy cutters" not far away. When the Tripoli struck the mine the sailors were not sure what had happened until they saw torrents of water flooding the ship. The flooding was brought under control, although the ship was dead in the water and out of action for quite some time. The USS *Trenton* took over for the *Tripoli* as a platform in the continuing mine-clearing operations.

The *Princeton* suffered major structural damage to its hull and propeller shaft. It also was left dead in the water and had to be towed back to Bahrain for repairs. Three sailors aboard the *Princeton* sustained injuries.

It has subsequently been revealed that repairs to the *Princeton* will run at least $56 million. It was also revealed that the ship came perilously close to breaking in two due to the structural damage to its hull.

American, British and Saudi minesweeping forces found another twenty-two mines in the general vicinity of the incidents. As of 20 February it was disclosed that allied forces had detected over 160 mines in the Gulf.

On 19 February it was announced that over 90 mines had been destroyed and another 90 waited to be neutralized. The United States accused the Iraqi government of violating the international rules of warfare by using free-floating mines in international shipping lanes. The use of free-floating mines in any waters is banned by the Geneva Convention as they are a total menace to all vessels regardless of nationality. In other words they are another form of international terrorism. The mines are relatively inexpensive while being quite effective and troublesome to remove or neutralize.

Before the ground war kicked off on 24 February the Navy's big gun platform got into position and started their shelling of Iraqi positions. These positions included ammunition dumps, mortar and artillery positions, supply and communications centers and armored units. Navy minesweepers cleared out special lanes so that the battleships could get in as close as possible to the shore.

The two battlewagons put on an impressive display of firepower. During a sixty-hour period from 23 to 26 February the gunners on the *Missouri* fired 595 shells on Iraqi tank and artillery positions on Faylaka Island off the coast of Kuwait City, as well as hitting targets in and about the Kuwait City airport.

Amphibious Decoys

The battleships succeeded in their second mission, which was to fool and confuse the Iraqi forces. The Iraqis were totally fooled into believing that the long-expected amphibious landing was imminent. In his news conference General Schwarzkopf stated, "It became very apparent to us early that the Iraqis were very concerned about an amphibious operation across the shores to liberate Kuwait."

Some 7,500 Marines were offloaded from the amphibious transports at the Saudi port of Jubail, but these forces did not constitute an invasion force. These troops operated in support of the 2nd Marine Division's thrust up the coast.

Even though the Marines who were embarked on the amphibious transports were kept at the ready through several days of standbys and highest state of readiness postures, they were never given the green light to go ashore.

The senior naval commanders have subsequently stated that they were prepared to make an amphibious assault, but as the ground campaign progressed with astounding success the longer they waited the more it became obvious that the amphibious assault was not necessary and was not going to happen. Said Admiral LaPlante, "The kids were disappointed [at not having to go] initially." He stated further that if the Army drive had stalled then there probably would have been an amphibious assault. "The landing was postponed—not cancelled."

According to General Schwarzkopf the amphibious force while embarked helped to pin down a force of up to eight Iraqi Divisions. This in itself was a major accomplishment. Thus the largest amphibious armada to have been assembled in recent times became the invasion that never happened.

In addition to the obvious reasons stated previously it was also felt by General Schwarzkopf that there would be too much collateral damage to civilian areas along the coastline of Kuwait if the Marines staged an amphibious assault. In establishing their defensive positions along the coast the Iraqi military set up defenses in civilian areas that the coalition forces would have had to blast their way through without regard to possible casualties, and they were not prepared to do that.

It was disclosed by Admiral LaPlante that had the 4th MEB (Marine Expeditionary Brigade) gone in, the Kuwaiti port of Ash Shuaybah was to have been their primary objective.

Even after the cease-fire the United Nations embargo has stayed in effect so the Maritime Interdiction effort has continued just as it had been, without any interruption.

To date over 8,500 ships have been challenged, 1,000 ships have been boarded and over one million tons of illegal cargo diverted. That includes weapons, military hardware, repair parts, and construction materials and equipment.

A Saudi national reflected in a pool of oil at the Manifah Bay area of Saudi Arabia. The effects of the deliberate oil spillage will be with us and the residents of the Persian Gulf for years to come. USCG/Kalnback

Chapter 6

The Aftermath

On 28 March 1991 the *John F. Kennedy* battle group returned to its homeport of Norfolk, Virginia. The ships sailed into the tidewater area with the *San Jacinto* tieing up pierside at about 1230. On the ships the crews stood to and manned the rails, as they always do when entering a port, especially when returning to their homeport. This time, though, it was different, and the crew knew it. They were returning from a deployment, but it was not just any deployment. It had been a wartime deployment. Maybe it was not the same as back in World War II when ships returned blackened by Kamakaze hits, with two thirds of their crews dead and injured, but it had been war nevertheless, and the crews were proud of their accomplishments.

Earlier in the morning on the *Wisconsin*, awards had been presented. Navy Commendation Medals and Letters of Commendation were presented to members of the crew. This scene was repeated on many of the returning ships.

On *Iwo Jima* the captain presented medals to about thirty individuals after the ship had departed Morehead City, North Carolina, and was en route to Norfolk.

On the *America* the awards were presented in person by the Secretary of the Navy Lawrence F. Garrett III. The "Sec Nav," as he is known, flew

All Aircraft of VF–14 make a pass over Oceana Naval Air Station prior to their landing. Arnold Meisner

in personally to make the presentations and welcome the ship back home. Said one sailor, "It's something a sailor can be proud of. Not every sailor gets a medal presented to him by the Secretary of the Navy." While some would be getting Navy Commendation Medals or Meritorious Achievement Awards, among those presented, all were eventually presented with the new Middle East Service Medal and the old National Service Medal now authorized by Congress.

The ships were surrounded by numerous small craft, privately owned commercial and pleasure craft loaded down with vociferous well-wishers. To the crews on the warships, it was a welcome sight, and they appreciated it.

The *San Jacinto* led the way and was followed by the *South Carolina, Biddle, Thomas Hart, Seattle* and the *John F. Kennedy*. Last, but certainly not least, was the battleship *Wisconsin*, which tied up pierside at 1630. In all an estimated 50,000 ecstatic family members were pierside to search for and greet their loved ones. Once the ships had tied up, the joyous mobs of well-wishers could no longer be restrained by the hard-pressed Navy security people. Whatever semblance of order and organization soon collapsed under the crush of families who had been separated for up to eight months.

In scenes that were to be repeated many times in the coming weeks the returning sailors were received as heroes. The first men off the ships were the new fathers, those sailors whose

107

wives had given birth to new sons and daughters while their fathers were at sea. Many proud fathers got the first glimpses of their new children on the pier that day. Throughout Norfolk there wasn't an empty motel room to be had, and all over the yellow ribbons of remembrance were hung along with red, white and blue. They were the colors of the day.

In Mayport, Florida, the *Saratoga* battle group returned at the same day and time that the ships returned to Norfolk. There the scene pierside was not any different.

The air wings had flown in to their respective home bases on the previous day. The scene at Oceana Naval Air Station was typical. Overhead the air wings roared in. First the entire formation made a pass over the assembled crowd before they landed individually. First VF-14, then VF-32, followed by the attack squadrons. They came in waves—first one unit then another. This went on from about 1330 until almost dusk with the daylight fading in the background.

Onboard the *Wisconsin* Sen. John Warner (Republican) from Virginia, himself a naval veteran of two wars, gave the crew a pep talk, telling them "now it's time to make love not war." Warner further recollected his own experiences

One of Kennedy's A–6E Intruder aircraft upon landing at Oceana. Note the bomb mission markings. Arnold Meisner

108

as a young sailor serving on a shore patrol detail on V-J Day.

Ten days later on 18 April, Amphibious Group Two returned to the naval base at Norfolk. The day before they had arrived at Morehead City, North Carolina, to disembark the Marines, and then sailed up to their homeport in Norfolk.

Greeting the *Iwo Jima* as it tied up in Morehead City, North Carolina, was the local high school band all decked out in its red and white uniforms. They sounded pretty good for a high school band. It was obvious that they had practiced for this one. One could tell they were playing with feeling, and when they broke into the "Star Spangled Banner" everyone came to a stop and stood at attention. Even to those who had only been away a short time it sounded good. Onboard the *Iwo Jima* the eyes were fixed on the forward jackstaff. The moment that the blue and white US Navy Ensign was hoisted the ship would cease to be under way. Then the whistle blew, and the Navy Jack was hoisted. They at long last were home.

There the scene pierside was much the same as it had been when the *Kennedy* battle group returned. In Morehead City and indeed the entire area surrounding Jacksonville, North Carolina, it was almost like a national holiday. The school children had been given the day off, and they, along with seemingly every able-bodied adult, lined the route of the troops back to Camp Lejune. With flags waving and cheering they welcomed their troops back home. Everywhere people were in a frenzy to make the returning soldiers and sailors, and subconsciously themselves, know that this time it was different.

The next day the USS *America* returned to Norfolk. Aircraft carrier homecomings are normally hectic affairs. This one was even more so: thousands of people all waiting for one person in particular. Once again it was the new fathers who made the first appearance, followed by those who were going on leave. Seemingly reluctantly, the ship disgorged its human cargo, slowly in a single file. The scene had become familiar—first the frenzied reunion when the relatives and loved ones found each other, then

more hugging and kissing pierside. And then, slowly and with a sense of relief with seabags and baby strollers in tow, the emotionally exhausted but exhilarated families made their way back to the family car or wherever they intended to go. The McDonald's that is pierside was packed. Big Macs were the order of the day.

Two days later the *Nassau* was the final amphibious ship to return. The spirits were high, not even the 5½ in. of rain could dampen the spirits of those who came to welcome their loved ones home.

In the Pacific the aircraft carrier *Midway* returned to her homeport of Yokosuka, Japan, and her air wing returned to Atsugi.

Welcome home! Lt. Perry Lucas of VF–14, his wife Lisa, and son Clayton Royal, whom he had never seen until that moment. Arnold Meisner/Defense Image

Back in the Persian Gulf the events continued to astound. The abortive Shiite and Kurdish uprisings against Saddam Hussein's brutal regime collapsed, resulting in tremendous social upheaval. Hundreds of thousands of Kurdish refugees took to the hills on the Iraqi-Turkish border. Operation Desert Storm became Operation Provide Comfort. While Desert Storm was over and CENTCOM was packing its bags, Provide Comfort was to be a EUCOM (European Command) affair.

The *Theodore Roosevelt* was deployed from the Persian Gulf to the eastern Mediterranean to provide air support for the American forces on the ground.

Stateside it was announced that the aircraft carrier *Forrestal*, soon to be withdrawn from active deployment to replace the old training carrier USS *Lexington*, was to make one last deployment to relieve the *Roosevelt* on station in the Mediterranean.

For the Navy Desert Storm and Desert Shield represent a high-water mark of American naval power, probably never to be achieved again. In a speech to Air Force personnel in Saudi Arabia Gen. Colin Powell said that Sad-

The return of the USS Wisconsin *to her homeport of Norfolk, Virginia.* Arnold Meisner/Defense Image

dam Hussein had to use his military machine or lose it. Something similar can be said about the US military.

Even while the battleships *Wisconsin* and *Missouri* were garnering the headlines, their sister ships *New Jersey* and *Iowa* were being decommissioned and laid up indefinitely, and plans to decommission the *Wisconsin* and *Missouri* were announced before those ships even returned home. While moves are afoot to give the *Missouri* a reprieve, it is only temporary and designed so as to enable it to participate in events to commemorate the 7 December attack by the Japanese on Pearl Harbor scheduled for later in 1991.

With the cancellation of the A-12 Avenger carrier stealth attack aircraft, as well as the F-14D, and the AX advanced attack aircraft still a doodle on the drawing board, the future of naval aviation is confused if not outright bleak. With the phasing out of the F-14 Tomcat, and its replacement with an improved FA-18 all that the Navy can expect in the line of aircraft procurement in the near future, the Navy's Carrier Air Wings will be taking on a leaner look.

At this point the big winner appears to be the Air Force with the award of an enormous contract to build the very impressive F-22 Lightning II. Tactical air supremacy for the Air Force seems assured for decades to come.

The throng of families waiting pierside for the return of the battleship Wisconsin. *Arnold Meisner/Defense Image*

One of the success stories of Desert Storm was the operation of active services backed up by the reserve structure. It worked with skill and professionalism.

Despite some problems the sealift performed surprisingly well when you consider its allegedly antiquated status and questionable state of readiness and availability. While there were problems—ships breaking down, ships not ready for sea when they were supposed to be and not enough professional crews available—the system, which many thought was just a scheme on paper and never ever thought would be actually used, functioned and functioned well. All the supplies and equipment reached their intended destinations. The prepositioned ships did exactly what they were supposed to do. Recent hearings have spotlighted the deficiencies in the system, and now planners are talking about increasing the national military sealift capability.

We were also lucky, in that there was no active threat to the ships en route as there had been in World War II. The Saudis had excellent port facilities, and the military in the field had extensive host nation support and logistics capabilities. This may not necessarily be true in the future.

The current situation seems to be one of contradiction—more will have to be done with less. Ships of the combat force that were still on

Family reunions were held on the deck of the Wisconsin. Arnold Meisner/Defense Image

station have already participated in two separate relief operations. Ships of the *Roosevelt* battle group and Sixth Fleet elements have provided support and supplies to Operation Provide Comfort (the relief of Kurdish refugees) while elements of the Third MEF (Marine Expeditionary Force) with the USS *Tarawa* have participated in operations to provide relief to victims and survivors of the massive typhoon that killed over 137,000 people and devastated the coast of Bangladesh.

Of the US Navy's ships that took part in Desert Storm the vast majority of them were from the Atlantic fleet. Four of the six aircraft carrier battle groups deployed were from the Atlantic fleet (*Saratoga, Kennedy, America* and *Roosevelt*), while only two were from the Pacific (*Ranger* and *Midway—Midway* being the forward deployed carrier, homeported in Japan). Of the three additional aircraft carriers being readied for Gulf deployment but never sent, two were Atlantic based (*Forrestal* and *Eisenhower*). *Nimitz* was the Pacific-based carrier. *Independence*, a Pacific-based carrier, was over there also but subsequently returned. Of the battleships the *Wisconsin*, which deployed in August, was from the Atlantic while *Missouri*, which did not deploy until after Christmas, was a Pacific-based ship. The largest of the amphibious groups, Amphibious Group Two with the 4th MEB em-

Marines onboard the USS Iwo Jima *cast an anxious eye toward the first landfall on their return to the* United States *after their participation in Desert Storm.* Arnold Meisner/Defense Image

barked, was from the Atlantic. Four of the Navy's carriers were not available for service: *Enterprise, Kitty Hawk, Constellation* and *Vinson*. All of these were undergoing some stage of extensive yard work. The United States has for most of this century maintained a two-ocean navy connected by a very thin canal through the Isthmus of Panama.

While it is obvious that there will be an increased naval presence in the Middle East for some time to come, how long the US Navy will be able to perform its many commitments around the world and answer to many more we do not yet know. In a period of reduced manpower, officer force-outs, reduced deployments and less steaming time the Navy will have to do more with less.

As part of the initial optimism after the phenomenal military success of Desert Storm, Middle East peace seems just as illusive now as it has ever been, as Secretary of State James Baker is finding out. Achieving a lasting regional peace is not going to be easy.

The Kuwaitis are beginning to dig themselves out of almost unbelievable devastation to their country and the environment, which has been deliberately poisoned and polluted almost beyond comprehension.

As the Naval Jack is raised on the Iwo Jima *the Marines know that they are home.* Arnold Meisner/Defense Image

*The first Marines set foot ashore after eight months at
sea onboard the* Iwo Jima. Arnold Meisner/Defense
Image

Previous page
The view from the flight deck of the USS America *as it ties up at the pier in Norfolk, Virginia. The crowd numbering in the thousands waits below.* Arnold Meisner/Defense Image

Amnesty International in a recent report claimed that over 120,000 Iraqi soldiers lost their lives and another 80,000 civilians, including over 50,000 Iraqi Kurds, died for a total of over 200,000, with a further 1,000 dying every week from malnutrition and disease. These figures may be high but because we did not maintain any sort of body count this time we do not have any other announced source of information on the matter. Amnesty International also claims that about 5,000 Kuwaiti civilians died during occupation by the Iraqi military. Mine clearing at sea and on land will take months, and the damage to the ecosystem may take years before it is restored to anything close to where it was before the war broke out.

Yes, we liberated Kuwait, and yes, we built a fragile coalition and made it work. We defended the right for the world to get reasonably cheap oil, and yes, we scored an amazingly quick and successful tactical and strategic victory. But what else have we gained besides the knowledge that our weapons work?

Electricians Mate Charles "Buddy" Neimeyer is inundated by relatives wielding Crazy String, a canned confetti-like substance, as he hugs his mother who has traveled to Norfolk, Virginia, from her home in Long Island, New York, to welcome him home. Arnold Meisner/Defense Image

118

International Warships in Gulf

Argentina
ARA *Almirante Brown*, destroyer
ARA *Spiro*, frigate

Australia
HMAS *Adelaide*, frigate
HMAS *Darwin*, frigate
HMAS *Success*, supply ship
HMAS *Sydney*, frigate
HMAS *Brisbane*, frigate
HMAS *Westfalia*, oiler

Belgium
Iris mine-countermeasures ship
Dianthus mine-countermeasures ship
Myasotis mine-countermeasures ship

Canada
HMCS *Athabaskan*, destroyer
HMCS Huron, destroyer
HMCS *Terra Nova*, destroyer escort
HMCS *Protector*, oiler

Denmark
Olfert Fischer, corvette

France
Clemenceau, aircraft carrier
Colbert, cruiser
Latouche-Treville, destroyer

Dupleix, destroyer
Duguay-Trouin, destroyer
Sufferen, destroyer
Durance, oiler
Eridan, mine-countermeasures ship
Orion, mine-countermeasures ship

Germany
2 mine-countermeasures ships

Greece
Limnos, frigate

Italy
Audace, destroyer
Lupo, frigate
San Marco, amphibious ship
Maestrale, frigate
Milazzo, mine-countermeasures ship
Sapri, mine-countermeasures ship
Vieste, mine-countermeasures ship
Tremiti, 1 support ship
Libeccio, frigate
Orsa, frigate
Stromboli, oiler

Japan
JMSDF *Yurishima*, mine-countermeasures
    ship
JMSDF *Hiroshima*, mine-countermeasures
    ship
JMSDF *Awashima*, mine-countermeasures
    ship

JMSDF *Sakashima*, mine-countermeasures
ship
JMSDF *Hayase*, mine-countermeasures
support ship
JMSDF *Tokiwa*, supply ship

The Netherlands
HrMs *Jacob van Heenskerck*, frigate
HrMs *Philips van Almonde*, frigate
HrMs *Zuiderkruis*, supply ship
HrMs Alkmaar, mine-countermeasures ship
HrMs Witte de With, frigate
HrMs Pieter Florisz, frigate

Norway
KNM *Andenes*, coast guard

Portugal
NRP *Sao Miguel*, supply ship
NRP *Comandante Sacaduro Cabral*, frigate
NRP *Comandante Roberto Ivens*, frigate

Spain
Santa Maria, frigate
Descubierra, frigate
Cazadona, frigate
Aragon, transport
Asturias, frigate
Reina Sofia, frigate
Numancia, frigate

United Kingdom
HMS *York*, destroyer
HMS *Battleaxe*, frigate
HMS *Jupiter*, frigate
HMS *Gloucester*, destroyer
HMS *Brazen*, frigate
HMS *London*, frigate
HMS *Cardiff*, destroyer
HMS *Atherstone*, mine-countermeasures ship
HMS *Catistock*, mine-countermeasures ship
HMS *Harworth*, mine-countermeasures ship
HMS *Herald*, survey ship
RFA *Fort Grange*, supply ship
RFA *Diligence*, repair ship
RFA *Olna*, oiler
RFA *Orange Leaf*, Oiler
RFA *Sir Galahad*, landing ship

RFA *Resource*, ammunition ship
RFA *Sir Percivale*, landing ship logistic
RFA *Sir Bedivere*, landing ship logistic
RFA *Sir Tristam*, landing ship logistic
RFA *Argus*, air training ship

United States

Eisenhower Battle Group
(April to October 1990)
USS *Dwight D. Eisenhower*, aircraft carrier,
CVN–69
USS *Ticonderoga*, guided-missile cruiser,
CG–47
USS *Scott*, guided-missile destroyer, DDG–995
USS *Tattnall*, guided-missile destroyer,
DDG–19
USS *John Rodgers*, destroyer, DD–983
USS *John L. Hall*, guided-missile frigate,
FFG–32
USS *Paul*, frigate, FF–1080
USS *Suribachi*, ammunition ship, AE–21
USS *Sierra*, destroyer tender, AD–18

Independence Battle Group
(June to 25 December 1990)
USS *Independence*, aircraft carrier, CV–62
USS *Jouett*, guided-missile cruiser, CG–29
USS *Goldsborough*, guided-missile destroyer,
DDG–20
USS *Brewton*, frigate, FF–1086
USS *Reasoner*, frigate, FF–1063
USS *Cimarron*, oiler, AO–177
USS *Flint*, ammunition ship, AE–32
USS *Antietam*, guided-missile cruiser, CG–54

Middle East Task Force
USS *LaSalle*, command ship, AGF–3
USS *England*, guided-missile cruiser, CG–22
USS *Vandergrift*, guided-missile frigate,
FFG–48
USS *Rentz*, guided-missile frigate, FFG–46
USS *Robert G. Bradley*, guided-missile frigate,
FFG–49
USS *Barbey*, frigate, FF–1088
USS *David R. Ray*, destroyer, DD–971
USS *Reid*, guided-missile frigate, FFG–30
USS *Blue Ridge*, amphibious command ship,
LCC–19

Saratoga Battle Group
(4 August 1990 to 28 March 1991)
USS *Saratoga*, aircraft carrier, CV-60
USS *Wisconsin*, battleship, BB-64
USS *Philippine Sea*, guided-missile cruiser, CG-58
USS *Biddle*, guided-missile cruiser, CG-34
USS *Sampson*, guided-missile destroyer, DDG-10
USS *Spruance*, destroyer, DD-963
USS *Elmer Montgomery*, frigate, FF-1082
USS *Thomas C. Hart*, frigate, FF-1092
USS *Detroit*, support ship, AOE-4
USS *Yellowstone*, destroyer tender, AD-41

Kennedy Battle Group
(14 August 1990 to 28 March 1991)
USS *John F. Kennedy*, aircraft carrier, CV-67
USS *San Jacinto*, guided-missile cruiser, CG-56
USS *Thomas S. Gates*, guided-missile cruiser, CG-51
USS *Mississippi*, guided-missile cruiser, CGN-40
USS *Samuel B. Roberts*, guided-missile frigate, FFG-58
USS *Sylvania*, stores ship, AFS-2
USS *Seattle*, support ship, AOE-3

Mine-Countermeasures Ships
USS *Avenger*, MCM-1
USS *Adroit*, MSO-509
USS *Impervious*, MSO-449
USS *Leader*, MSO-490

Theodore Roosevelt Battle Group
(28 December 1990 to 28 June 1991)
USS *Theodore Roosevelt*, aircraft carrier, CVN-71
USS *Leyte Gulf*, guided-missile cruiser, CG-55
USS *Richmond K. Turner*, guided-missile cruiser, CG-20
USS *Caron*, destroyer, DD-970
USS *Hawes*, guided-missile frigate, FFG-53
USS *Vreeland*, frigate, FF-1069
USS *Platte*, oiler, AO-186
USS *Santa Barbara*, ammunition ship, AE-28

America Battle Group
(28 December 1990 to 8 April 1991)
USS *America*, aircraft carrier, CV-66

USS *Normandy*, guided-missile cruiser, CG-60
USS *Virginia*, guided-missile cruiser, CGN-38
USS *Preble*, guided-missile destroyer, DDG-46
USS *William V. Pratt*, guided-missile destroyer, DDG-44
USS *Halyburton*, guided-missile frigate, FFG-40
USS *Kalamazoo*, oiler, AOR-6
USS *Nitro*, ammunition ship, AE-23

Ranger Battle Group
(deployed 8 December 1990)
USS *Ranger*, aircraft carrier, CV-61
USS *Valley Forge*, guided-missile cruiser, CG-50
USS *Princeton*, guided-missile cruiser, CG-59
USS *Horne*, guided-missile cruiser, CG-30
USS *Harry W. Hill*, destroyer, DD-986
USS *Paul F. Foster*, destroyer, DD-964
USS *Jarrett*, guided-missile frigate, FFG-33
USS *Francis Hammond*, frigate, FF-1067
USS *Kansas City*, oiler, AOR-3
USS *Shasta*, ammunition ship, AE-33

Midway Battle Group
(October 1990 to March 1991)
USS *Midway*, aircraft carrier, CV-41
USS *Mobile Bay*, guided-missile cruiser, CG-53
USS *Bunker Hill*, guided-missile cruiser, CG-52
USS *Fife*, destroyer, DD-991
USS *Oldendorf*, destroyer, DD-972
USS *Hewitt*, destroyer, DD-966
USS *Curts*, guided-missile frigate, FFG-38
USS *San Jose*, stores ship, AFS-7

Amphibious Ships
USS *Okinawa*, assault ship, LPH-3
USS *Ogden*, transport dock ship, LPD-5
USS *Durham*, cargo ship, LKA-114
USS *Fort McHenry*, landing ship dock, LSD-43
USS *Cayuga*, landing ship tank, LST-1186

Marine Amphibious Readiness Group
(with *Saratoga* Battle Group)
USS *Inchon*, assault ship, LPH-12
USS *Nashville*, transport dock ship, LPD-13
USS *Whidbey Island*, landing ship dock, LSD-41
USS *Newport*, landing ship tank, LST-1179

USS *Fairfax County*, landing ship tank, LST-1193

Amphibious Group 2
(with 4th Marine Expeditionary Brigade)
USS *Nassau*, assault ship, LHA-4
USS *Guam*, assault ship, LPH-9
USS *Iwo Jima*, assault ship, LPH-2
USS *Shreveport*, transport dock ship, LPD-12
USS *Raleigh*, transport dock ship, LPD-1
USS *Trenton*, transport dock ship, LPD-14
USS *Pensacola*, landing ship dock, LSD-38
USS *Portland*, landing ship dock, LSD-37
USS *Gunston Hall*, landing ship dock, LSD-44
USS *Saginaw*, landing ship tank, LST-1188
USS *Spartanburg County*, landing ship tank, LST-1192
USS *Manitowoc*, landing ship tank, LST-1180
USS *La Moure County*, landing ship tank, LST-1194

Amphibious Group 3
(with 5th Marine Expeditionary Brigade)
USS *Tarawa*, assault ship, LHA-1
USS *Tripoli*, assault ship, LPH-10
USS *New Orleans*, assault ship, LPH-11
USS *Vancouver*, transport dock ship, LPD-2
USS *Denver*, transport dock ship, LPD-9
USS *Juneau*, transport dock ship, LPD-10
USS *Anchorage*, landing ship dock, LSD-36
USS *Germantown*, landing ship dock, LSD-42
USS *Mount Vernon*, landing ship dock, LSD-39
USS *Mobile*, cargo ship, LKA-115
USS *Barbour County*, landing ship tank, LST-1195
USS *Frederick*, landing ship tank, LST-1184
USS *Peoria*, landing ship tank, LST-1183

Missouri Battle Group
USS *Missouri*, battleship, BB-63
USS *Sacramento*, support ship, AOE-1
USS *Ford*, guided-missile frigate, FFG-54

Additional Ships
USN *Louisville*, attack submarine, SSN-724
USN *Pittsburgh*, attack submarine, SSN-720
USN *Mars*, stores ship, AFS-1
USN *Niagara Falls*, stores ship, AFS-3
USN *San Diego*, stores ship, AFS-6

USS *White Plains*, stores ship, AFS-4
USS *Sterret*, guided-missile cruiser, CG-31
USS *Vandergrift*, guided-missile frigate, FFG-48
USS *Taylor*, guided-missile frigate, FFG-50
USS *South Carolina*, guided-missile cruiser, CGN-37
USS *Worden*, guided-missile cruiser, CG-18
USS *Leftwich*, destroyer, DD-984
USS *Kidd*, guided-missile destroyer, DDG-993
USS *MacDonough*, guided-missile destroyer, DDG-39
USS *McInerney*, guided-missile frigate, FFG-8
USS *Nicholas*, guided-missile frigate, FFG-47
USS *Marvin Shields*, frigate, FF-1066
USS *Acadia*, destroyer tender, AD-42
USS *Haleakala*, ammunition ship, AE-25
USS *Kiska*, ammunition ship, AE-35
USS *Mount Hood*, ammunition ship, AE-29
USS *Vulcan*, repair ship, AR-5
USS *Jason*, repair ship, AR-8
USS *Beaufort*, salvage and rescue ship, ATS-2

Hospital Ships
USS *Mercy*, T-AH-20
USS *Comfort*, T-AH-19

Fast Sealift Ships
USNS *Algol*, T-AKR-287
USNS *Bellatrix*, T-AKR-288
USNS *Denebola*, T-AKR-289
USNS *Pollux*, T-AKR-290
USNS *Altair*, T-AKR-291
USNS *Regulus*, T-AKR-292
USNS *Capella*, T-AKR-293
USNS *Antares*, T-AKR-294

Maritime Prepositioned Ships
USNS *Cpl. Louis J. Hauge*, T-AK-3000
USNS *Pfc. William B. Baug*, T-AK-3001
USNS *Pfc. James Anderson, Jr.*, T-AK-3002
USNS *1st Lt. Alex Bonnyman, Jr.*, T-AK-3003
USNS *Pvt. Harry Fisher*, T-AK-3004
USNS *Sgt. Matej Kocak*, T-AK-3005
USNS *Pfc. Eugene Obregon*, T-AK-3006
USNS *Maj. Stephen W. Pless*, T-AK-3007
USNS *2nd Lt. John P. Bobo*, T-AK-3008
USNS *Pfc. DeWayne T. Williams*, T-AK-3009
USNS *1st Lt. Baldomero Lopez*, T-AK-3010

USNS *1st Lt. Jack Lummus*, T-AK-3011
USNS *Sgt. William R. Button*, T-AK-3012

Afloat Prepositioning Ships
USNS *American Kestrel*, T-AK-2043
USNS *Austral Rainbow*, T-AK-2046
USNS *Green Island*, T-AK-1015
USNS *Green Harbour*, T-AK-2064

USNS *Advantage*, T-AK-2040
USNS *Noble Star*, T-AK-5076
USNS *Santa Victoria*, T-AK-1010
USNS *Overseas Alive*, T-AOT-1203
USNS *Overseas Valdez*, T-AOT-1204
USNS *Overseas Vivian*, T-AOT-1205
USNS *Sealift Pacific*, T-AOT-169
USNS *American Cormorant*, T-AK-2062

Appendix 2

Carrier Air Wing Deployment

USS *Dwight D. Eisenhower*, Carrier Air Wing 7

Squadron	Name	Aircraft	Base
VF-142	Ghostriders	F-14A+	Oceana, VA
VF-143	Puckin' Dogs	F-14A+	Oceana, VA
VFA-131	Wildcats	FA-18	Cecil Field, FL
VFA-136	Knighthawks	FA-18	Cecil Field, FL
VA-34	Blue Blasters	A-6E, KA-6D	Oceana, VA
VAW-121	Bluetails	E-2C	Norfolk, VA
VAQ-140	Patriots	EA-6B	Whidbey Island, WA
VS-31	Top Cats	S-3B	Cecil Field, FL
HS-5	Night Dippers	SH-3H	Jacksonville, FL

USS *Independence*, Carrier Air Wing 14

Squadron	Name	Aircraft	Base
VF-21	Freelancers	F-14	Miramar, CA
VF-154	Black Knights	F-14	Miramar, CA
VFA-25	Fists of the Fleet	FA-18C	Lemore, CA
VFA-113	Stingers	FA-18C	Lemore, CA
VA-196	Main Battery	A-6E	Whidbey Island, WA
VAW-113	Black Eagles	E-2C	Miramar, CA
VAQ-139	Cougars	EA-6B	Whidbey Island, WA
VS-37	Sawbucks	S-3A	North Island, CA
HS-8	Eight Ballers	SH-3H	North Island, CA

USS *John F. Kennedy*, Carrier Air Wing 3

Squadron	Name	Aircraft	Base
VF-14	Tophatters	F-14A	Oceana, VA
VF-32	Swordsmen	F-14A	Oceana, VA
VA-45	Clansmen	A-7E	Cecil Field, FL
VA-72	Bluehawks	A-7E	Cecil Field, FL
VA-75	Sunday Punchers	A-6E, KA-6D	Oceana, VA
VAW-126	Seahawks	E-2C	Norfolk, VA
VAQ-130	Zappers	A-6B	Whidbey Island, WA
VS-22	Checkmates	S-3B	Cecil Field, FL
HS-7	Shamrocks	SH-3H	Jacksonville, FL

USS *Midway*, Carrier Air Wing 5

Squadron	Name	Aircraft	Base
VFA-151	Vigilantes	FA-18A	Atsugi, Japan
VFA-192		FA-18A	Atsugi, Japan
VFA-195		FA-18A	Atsugi, Japan
VA-115	Eagles	A-6E, KA-6D	Atsugi, Japan
VA-185	Nighthawks	A-6E, KA-6D	Atsugi, Japan
VAW-115	Sentinels	E-2C	Atsugi, Japan
VAQ-136	Gauntlets	EA-6B	Atsugi, Japan
HS-12	Wyverns	SH-3H	Atsugi, Japan

USS *Ranger*, Carrier Air Wing 2

Squadron	Name	Aircraft	Base
VF-1	Wolfpack	F-14A	Miramar, CA
VF-2	Bounty Hunters	F-14A	Miramar, CA
VA-145	Swordsmen	A-6E	Whidbey Island, WA
VA-155	Silver Foxes	A-6E	Whidbey Island, WA
VAW-116	Sun Kings	E-2C	Miramar, CA
VAQ-131	Lancers	EA-6B	Whidbey Island, WA
VS-28	Hurkers	S-3A	North Island, CA
HS-14		SH-3H	North Island, CA

USS *Saratoga*, Carrier Air Wing 17

Squadron	Name	Aircraft	Base
VF-74	Bedevilers	F-14A+	Oceana, VA
VF-103	Sluggers	F-14A+	Oceana, VA
VF/A-31	Rampagers	FA-18C	Cecil Field, FL
VF/A-81	Sunliners	FA-18C	Cecil Field, FL
VA-35	Black Panthers	A-6E, KA-6D	Oceana, VA
VAW-125	Tiger Tails	E-2C	Norfolk, VA
VAQ-132	Scorpions	EA-6B	Whidbey Island, WA
VS-30	Diamond Cutters	S-3B	Cecil Field, FL
HS-3	Tridents	SH-3H	Jacksonville, FL

USS *America,* Carrier Air Wing 1

Squadron	Name	Aircraft	Base
VF-33	Starfighters	F-14A	Oceana, VA
VF-102	Diamondbacks	F-14A	Oceana, VA
VFA-82		FA-18C	Cecil Field, FL
VFA-86		FA-18C	Cecil Field, FL
VA-85	Black Falcons	A-6E, KA-6D	Oceana, VA
VAW-123	Screwtops	E-2C	Norfolk, VA
VAQ-137	Kestrels	EA-6B	Whidbey Island, WA
VS-32	Maulers	S-3B	Cecil Field, FL
HS-11	Dragon Slayers	SH-3H	Jacksonville, FL

USS *Theodore Roosevelt,* Carrier Air Wing 8

Squadron	Name	Aircraft	Base
VF-41	Black Aces	F-14A	Oceana, VA
VF-84	Jolly Rogers	F-14A	Oceana, VA
VFA-15		FA-18A	Cecil Field, FL
VFA-87		FA-18A	Cecil Field, FL
VA-36	Road Runners	A-6E	Oceana, VA
VA-65	Tigers	A-6E	Oceana, VA
VAW-124	Bear Aces	E-2C	Norfolk, VA
VAQ-141	Shadowhawks	EA-6B	Whidbey Island, WA
VS-24	Duty Cats	B-3B	Cecil Field, FL
HS-9	Sea Griffins	SH-3H	Jacksonville, FL

Index

126

About the Author
Arnold Meisner is a photojournalist and writer specializing in US Navy affairs. His photographs have appeared in books, magazines and newspapers around the world. He is coauthor, with Dennis Bailey, of a forthcoming book on the US Navy's Aegis guided-missile cruisers, also published by Motorbooks International. Meisner lives in Peaks Island, Maine. *Photo by Dennis Finley*

Now from Motorbooks International, The POWER Series provides an in-depth look at the troops, weapon systems, ships, planes, machinery and missions of the world's modern military forces. From training to battle action, the top military units are detailed and illustrated with top quality color and black and white photography.

Available through book shops and specialty stores or direct. Call toll free 1-800-826-6600. From overseas 715-294-3345 or fax 715-294-4448

AIRBORNE: Assault from the Sky—
by Hans Halberstadt
America's front line parachute divisions

AIR GUARD: America's Flying Militia—
by George Hall
From the cockpit on their flying missions

ARMY AVIATION—by Hans Halberstadt
American power house; how it evolved, how it works

DESERT SHIELD: The Build-up; The Complete Story—by Robert F. Dorr
All the action leading up to Operation Desert Storm

DESERT STORM AIR WAR—
by Robert F. Dorr
Blow-by-blow account of the allied air force and naval air campaign to liberate Kuwait

DESERT STORM GROUND WAR—
by Hans Halberstadt
Soldier's-eye view of the allied ground victory over Iraq

CV: Carrier Aviation—
by Peter Garrison and George Hall
Directly from the flight deck

GREEN BERETS: Unconventional Warriors—by Hans Halberstadt
"To liberate from oppression"

ISRAEL'S ARMY—by Samuel M. Katz
Inside this elite modern fighting force

ISRAEL'S AIR FORCE
by Samuel M. Katz
Inside the world's most combat-proven air force

MARINE AIR: First to Fight—
by John Trotti and George Hall
America's most versatile assault force

NTC: A Primer of Modern Mechanized Combat—by Hans Halberstadt
The US National (Tank and Helicopter) Training Center

STRIKE: US Naval Strike Warfare Center—
by John Joss and George Hall
US Navy's "Top Gun" for ground attack pilots

TANK ATTACK: A Primer of Modern Tank Warfare—
by Steven J. Zaloga and Michael Green
American tanks and tactics in the 1990s

TOP GUN: The Navy's Fighter Weapons School—by George Hall
The best of the best

USCG: Always Ready—by Hans Halberstadt
Coast Guard search and rescue, Alaska patrol and more

SPACE SHUTTLE: The Quest Continues—
by George J. Torres
Pre-shuttle and shuttle operations history

More titles are constantly in preparation